the sandbox revolution

raising kids for a just world

edited by lydia wylie-kellermann

BROADLE
MINNEA.

THE SANDBOX REVOLUTION
Raising Kids for a Just World

Cover image and design: Joel Holland

Print ISBN: 978-1-5064-6644-6
eBook ISBN: 978-1-5064-6645-3

For all the children who have inspired the writing and the reading of this book. May you know you are loved in freedom and fullness. And may there always be laughter and dancing and justice.

Contents

Part 1 Nitty-Gritty Decisions as Radical Practices

Part 2 Confronting the "Isms" in Our Families

Part 3 Reclaiming Community

Your children are not your children.
They are the sons and daughters
of Life's longing for itself.
They come through you but not from you,
And though they are with you
yet they belong not to you.
You may give them your love
but not your thoughts,
For they have their own thoughts.
You may house their bodies
but not their souls,
For their souls dwell in the house
of tomorrow,
which you cannot visit,
not even in your dreams.
You may strive to be like them,
but seek not to make them like you.

—Kahlil Gibran, *The Prophet*

Introduction

Questions That Ache

Lydia Wylie-Kellermann

Lydia Wylie-Kellermann is a writer, editor, activist, and mother. She lives with her partner and two boys in the neighborhood where she grew up in southwest Detroit. She is the managing editor of *Geez* magazine, a quarterly, ad-free print magazine at the intersection of art, activism, and faith. She is a contributor to multiple books, including *Rally: Litanies for the Lovers of God and Neighbor* (edited by Brittney Winn Lee, Upper Room Books, 2020); *Watershed Discipleship: Reinhabiting Bioregional Faith and Practice* (edited by Ched Myers, Cascade, 2016); and *Bury the Dead: Stories of Death and Dying, Resistance and Discipleship* (edited by Laurel Dykstra, Cascade, 2013).

We stand at a time of unraveling. All that lies just below the surface is being uncovered. The systems that have nursed us all our lives (capitalism, militarism, racism, individualism, etc.) are crumbling. And it is a beautiful thing because these systems are and have always been destructive to our global community of humans, creatures, and elements. We need this time of transformation, but the collapse is painful.

At night, I climb into my kids' bunk bed to snuggle beside them as they each name and hold their own fears. I put my hand on their backs and feel their bodies relax. I run my fingers through their hair and their heartbeats steady. I breathe my prayers into them as I feel them drift into dreams. I rest a little longer beside my sleeping boys, under the warmth of their covers, and I begin to weep for them, for our neighborhood, for the world. I feel the urgent temptation to shield them from it all. I could withhold the truth. I could take what privilege I have and use it to build a wall around us all.

But in reality, those temptations do not mirror my prayers. I want both my children to be fully human. I want them to know what it feels like to be alive. I want them to delight in the reciprocity of being communal members on this sweet Earth. And that means giving space for their hearts to break, honoring their hard questions, and encouraging them to act out of their own beliefs and passions.

Each of us reading these words has been made for this moment as an individual but also as one who is intertwined in the lives of children. We have been invited into this time of sacred shifting, which must move us from corporate, globalized systems that deal in death to localized, communal systems that nurture life. It is in this time and space that we all are nurturing children and being prodded by their laughter, fears, and questions.

There are moments in our daily monotony that seem to link the enormous love I have for these kids and my deep longings for justice. The intersection of those proddings consistently asks me to reevaluate how I live, what I believe in, and how big I dare to dream for what is possible for our communities.

A Bunny Funeral

Last summer, a pile of freshly dug dirt lay next to the hole in our backyard. My younger son, Cedar, then three, picked up the furry body of the beloved rabbit he had named Raccoon. He cuddled the stiff body in his arms as if it were a baby. He walked slowly around the circle of gathered family and neighbors, stopping to let each person say goodbye and pet Raccoon one last time. Then, with tears in his eyes, Cedar laid the body in the hole.

I stood under our grapevines with an aching heart for my boy. I was amazed at the sacred spirit he could hold and his tears that flowed freely. And I wondered, *How can those of us who love him nurture spaces that allow him, as he grows, to keep touching death and grief in a culture that tries to push death out of sight? How can we make sure he always feels freedom to cry and act tenderly? How can I resist the toxic masculinity that will be thrust upon him from every direction as he gets older?*

Hiding from Bears

It was just weeks into preschool when I picked up Isaac, my older son, from school. We piled into the car and buckled boosters and car seats as Isaac blurted out the stories from his day.

"Mommy, today at school, we had to lock the doors and all hide in the bathroom and be really quiet."

"Oh yeah, why did you have to do that?"

"In case a bear comes and wants to eat us."

Isaac had been told that lockdown drills were to protect him from bloodthirsty bears lurking around southwest Detroit. I didn't envy his teacher's job. How else do you explain to a four-year-old that our country cares more about money and owning guns than it does about the lives of our children? Now at seven, Isaac is taught to hide quietly from "bad guys with guns."

How on earth do we parent in an age when gun violence is so rampant in this country? How do we work to let our kids feel safe enough to grow and learn? How do we offer different narratives from "bad guys with guns"? How do we foster spaces where security is dependent on community, trust, and nonviolence rather than armed security guards and metal detectors?

Ultrasound Anxiety

Before either of these beloved children was born, I sat in the ultrasound room—not once, but twice—with goop on my belly and anxiety in my heart. I was shocked that I would be the mother of two boys. I never doubted for a second that I would love them. But I doubted my ability to be any good at it. I felt completely unprepared. I had been ready to raise powerful, smart, spirit-driven, feminist girls! But boys? And I was thrown off by my reaction, because of course I believe that gender is a social construct. So why the feelings of fear and insecurity?

The reality forced me to ask, What does it mean to raise two white boys in a world seeping with patriarchy and white supremacy? How will I teach them to take up less space, to listen first and deeply, and to trust the leadership of women and people of color? And on the other hand, how will I tend to their spirits and encourage them to be fully human in a system that threatens to destroy their souls? How will I invite them into the work of smashing this system and loving the hard work of resistance that will liberate us all?

Roots of the Maple

Those early fears are hard to remember as I stand in awe of the beautiful boys before me. On a recent spring day, I felt the warm dirt on my fingers as I readied the soil for baby kale and broccoli plants. As I worked, I watched Isaac a few beds away. He had found a maple seedling growing where the tomatoes would soon dwell. He knew the little tree couldn't grow there, but he couldn't bear to pull it out and throw it into the compost. He spent more than an hour in total concentration gently pulling the dirt away from the roots, which already reached down a full foot. At last, he tenderly pulled out the tree with every root intact. He moved it by an old stump where Grandpa thought it would be safe. He put the little tree back in the earth and watered her roots.

The love this kid has for the earth and her creatures melts my heart. I hold onto that love as I scroll through scientific studies that predict human extinction, perhaps even in my children's lifetime. This reality can knock the wind out of me. How do we raise kids who may very well see massive death and destruction of creatures, people, and the environment? What skills will they need? How do we help them keep loving and living in communion with the trees and the earthworms? How do we do anything but weep?

Tell Me Some Stories

I have so many questions that ache deep in my being. They are there when I harvest raspberries with my four-year-old. They are there when I drop my boys off at school. They are there when I choose what songs to sing to them at night. They are there when we march in the streets.

The answers to these questions are little and big, personal and systemic, and they impact the generations to come. I needed to know there are more people out there struggling with these questions. I needed stories that could offer company, wisdom, and truth in places I could not see.

So I began this most selfish of projects. I reached out to parents and grandparents whom I love and whose lives have inspired my footsteps. And I said, "Tell me some stories. Speak vulnerably. Help remind us of the wide community of which we are all a part."

And that is how the book you hold in your hands came to be.

The authors in this anthology are people who have the fire for justice in their bellies and are bringing their children alongside in the work. With a love for this world and a commitment to its future, parenting becomes a radical act of resistance and hope.

Parenting and activism are not separate; they mingle and prod us in unexpected ways.

Each contributor's life is a tapestry woven with many threads—diapers and demonstrations, prom dresses and prophetic wisdom. It all intersects in the ordinary and extraordinary work of believing in a just world.

With Tenderness and Imagination

I started dreaming this book in the many months of sleep deprivation during my sons' early years. Crying babies that never allowed me more than an hour and a half of uninterrupted sleep left me feeling never quite human. Parenting is the hardest thing I have ever done. It is exhausting, messy, isolating, and often very lonely.

We desperately need one another. We need one another to do a load of dishes, to rub our aching backs, and to laugh with us at our mistakes. We need to remind one another that we are not alone in our fears, our grief, and our hope. We need one another's hands to hold as we look with despair at this world and the future that we will give our children. We need one another's courage and imagination as we experiment with ways to live humanly.

This book is intended to be a thread in that web of companionship and support.

As we were writing these chapters, many of the authors gathered for a retreat. We joked that we should insert a chapter within these pages that says simply, "Take a nap." This is a book filled with love and permission to care for yourself. These words are not here to judge your parenting, or tell you there is one right way, or make you feel like you aren't doing enough. You are doing enough. Everything written on these pages is here only in the spirit of love, as an offering to all of us who yearn for a world of wild wonder and liberation. The words are here for you as you need them or when you get to them—like little gifts to be found between the loads of laundry or excruciating tantrums or time on swings and slides.

May these pages be covered with applesauce and breast milk, sand and slime, sweat and tears. May they push us into necessary discomfort. May they inspire small shifts in our patterns—or compel us to uproot our lives and change course.

May we always choose truth-telling. May we act with our lives. May we lift the beloved children in our lives onto our shoulders and together grab hold of that arc, bending it a little more toward justice in this hour and every hour.

A Note on Power, Process, and Accountability

As I begin to write these words, beeswax drips onto my desk. It is the final melting inches of a long, skinny candle first lit months ago, as summer gave way to an autumn breeze. It glowed in the center of our circle as a majority of the contributors to this book gathered for a weekend to build community, read one another's work, rest, write, and articulate common commitments for this book.

As writers, we know that words are powerful. They can change the course of history for the better. But they can also cause pain and replicate systems of oppression—consciously or unconsciously. Our hope is that the words on these pages are gifts that honor the communities we love.

Collectively, we want to be accountable to those who are on the front lines of the struggle, who are face-to-face with systems of terror. We understand that some of us have a deeper responsibility to seek accountability due to the social power and privilege we carry.

We want to be held accountable. So as we gathered, we asked ourselves and one another these questions:

To whom do you want to be—and feel we should
be—accountable?

On what issues do we as individual writers seek
accountability?

On what issues do we want others to be accountable?

What does accountability in writing and the creative
process mean?

Who is missing in this circle and in the book?

These conversations altered the course of *The Sandbox Revolution*. We committed to speaking honestly to one another about the places we needed to dig deeper or become more explicit. We agreed to make clear our social location in our writing. We wrote a list of values we shared for the book and asked a few readers, designated and compensated, to help us discern whether we were living up to them.

Our hope is that all readers will glimpse a bit of themselves on these pages and that all will also be stretched by the lives and words they may find unfamiliar.

We also want to add a note about our children. We want our words to be accountable to them. We want these stories to honor and love them, not harm or embarrass. So we committed as much as possible to sharing our work with our kids and securing their permission. Some writers explained their writing verbally to younger kids, and older kids read it. We even invited them to respond with pieces of their own if they wanted to. You will see that one did.

So now we send this book out into the world, knowing that writing is powerful and dangerous work. We have certainly made mistakes, run into limits, and followed unconscious privileged biases. We welcome your pushback, your critique, your pain—for it helps us all move toward justice.

Our process was not perfect, but it was honest and meaningful. Trust that every word in this book was written with love for our children and the world. Trust in the power of stories. Trust that we, too, are very human and that we are grateful to be in this messy, beautiful work with you.

Part 1

Nitty-Gritty Decisions as Radical Practices

These are the times to grow our souls. Each of us is called upon to embrace the conviction that despite the powers and principalities bent on commodifying all our human relationships, we have the power within us to create the world anew.

—Grace Lee Boggs, "Seeds of Change"

I could feel Isaac's heart beating as I held his hand and we walked through the door for his first day of first grade. As we entered his classroom, it was clear something wasn't right. All the parents had stayed with their children and had dazed expressions on their faces. Then I realized why: there was no teacher.

For weeks, they had only a substitute teacher who yelled and threatened and never seemed to teach. It eventually became clear that no teacher was coming and we needed to find another school for Isaac. But where?

Our lives turned upside down as my partner, Erinn, and I tried to figure out the next right thing. It was a personal decision that would affect the well-being of our child, and yet it lived in a systemic context. So we tried to make the expedient decision as carefully as possible, in regular communication with parents of Isaac's classmates. How do we trust our kids to neighborhood schools while the state is systemically destroying public education in Detroit?

It feels as though virtually every decision we make for our children has political ramifications. Where do they go to school? Where do we live? What food do we put in their bodies? How do we navigate the health care industry? How do we spend our money? And then, of course, there is the issue of who has choice in these matters and who doesn't. We can pretend these decisions are isolated and individual, but the truth is, we live in a web of systemic injustice. Our actions build or destroy community, interrupt or replicate oppressive patterns, and affect how our children will stand in the face of the powers in the future.

So in this first section, we examine those nitty-gritty, everyday decisions we make as parents and offer them as opportunities for radical practice.

1

What Makes a Family?

Infertility, Masculinity, and the Fecundity of Grace

Nick Peterson

Nick Peterson is husband to NaKisha, father to twin boys Zayden and Zander, and a doctoral student at Emory University in Atlanta. He spends most of his time thinking and writing about the complex relationship between Christian practices and anti-Blackness. His teaching focuses on the pastoral and ministerial arts of preaching and worship. He is an ordained itinerant deacon in the African Methodist Episcopal Church and serves on the ministerial staff at his local church.

Families are these complex units of people who may or may not share blood relations. By thinking of our families as opportunities for inclusion and embrace, we avail ourselves of possibilities we might not have imagined otherwise. Our families may not look like the plans we initially had, but the plot turns and twists are what make family meaningful and vital for our thriving.

All in the Family

My momma's parents lived around the corner from us when I was growing up. Like many Black folks, they were part of the great migration from the Deep South to the urban North and Midwest after the Second World War. My grandma came from working tobacco farms in Arkansas, while my grandfather tagged along with his older brother when he left Mississippi.

My grandparents were what I call "hands-on" people. They fished and hunted with their hands, cut grass and tended gardens with their hands, cooked everything from scratch with their hands, made clothes and doodads with their hands. And most of all, they loved on the world with their hands. They used their hands and their home to nurture and care for people. They made family possible with their loving hands.

For most of my childhood, my grandparents took care of my grandma's parents, Granddaddy Roscoe and Grandma Suzi. And when they passed, my grandparents started taking in children. We introduced them to all the kids in the neighborhood as our cousins, not as foster kids. We didn't know who Foster was, so it didn't make sense to us to introduce them as Foster's kids. For more than a decade, my grandparents took in many children, loving them into our family and giving them the best of care.

I don't think my grandparents understood at the time the example they were setting for the rest of our family. As adults, five of my mom's eight siblings would follow their parents' footsteps and take in children. I grew up with as many foster and adoptive cousins as blood cousins. My mom actually retired early from her job because she felt called to be a foster parent, specifically

4

for children with special needs. She was an advocate, therapist, mother, sister, auntie, teacher, and confidant to her foster children. She loved them into wholeness and adulthood, seeing to it that they would not fall through the cracks of the child welfare system and be left without support.

This notion of an extended and inclusive family was also present on my dad's side. His parents informally adopted his younger sister's best friends, a set of twins, when their mother died unexpectedly. It was years before we found out they were not our blood relatives. My dad's parents, too, cared for the generation that came before them. My dad's grandmother, Grandma Mo, lived with them for most of my childhood and helped take care of us as babies. And my great-aunt Velma, my grandmother's dad's sister, lived with them during my teenage years. At other times, my grandmother took in folks from our church who had fallen on hard times or who were recovering from illness.

Our family events on both sides were always a mix of blood family and "made" family. Home as a capacious site for care and compassion determined family, not blood alone. It was shared laughter and tears, shared joy and pain, shared offense and forgiveness that connected the various tiles of personality into a beautiful mosaic.

Titles like uncle, auntie, and cousin were not just about respect but ways to affirm the ability to *make* family, to extend love's reach and claim others as our own—to nurture family into existence. I loved that our family was large, with ambiguous borders that made my uncles' and aunts' closest friends our uncles and aunts and their kids our cousins. Little did I know how valuable and important these expansive notions of kinship and care I learned from my childhood would be for me as an adult.

(In)fertility

When my wife and I started dating after we finished college in Pennsylvania, we were excited to learn that we shared a wide and robust definition of family. Her mom had informally adopted a friend's daughter when her friend died after a short illness, and her dad has never met a stranger. He made family at the bowling alley for more than three decades, and I am pretty sure he has no more than three degrees of separation from any Black person in DC.

So it was no surprise that we, too, wanted a big family. We figured we would have some kids and adopt some. Even though we lived in Pennsylvania and our families were elsewhere, we had learned well the art of creating family. We developed close-knit, intergenerational relationships that provided the structure and support that makes family. Our friends in Pennsylvania joined us for family gatherings in DC and stayed with and visited my parents when they traveled through St. Louis.

Though we were not in a rush to have children, my wife and I were never consistent with any form of birth control, and for a while, we felt lucky for not getting pregnant. But about a year and a half in, it became our explicit intention to conceive. Yet her period kept coming—no pregnancy. My wife's doctor suggested that we try tracking her ovulation cycle for a full year, and we left feeling confident.

That year came and went—still no pregnancy. The doctor ordered a series of tests. My first test was a semen analysis. There was some awkwardness, having to go into the special bathroom with the small "collection door," but I felt pretty sure things would come back fine. I had given it my best shot.

When the results were abnormal, I was taken aback, to say the least. My male ego had assumed that "the issue" would be with my wife. It had not even crossed my mind that my sperm—or lack thereof—would be the problem. I had to wait another ninety days before a second test. Same result: no viable sperm in the sample. I was terrified. I was ashamed and felt humiliated—not because of anything my wife did or did not say to me, but because of what it meant to me to be a man who "shot blanks."

Male bodies are not subject to the same kind of invasive medical procedures to which female bodies are. For men, the most awkward part of a physical exam is the turn-your-head-and-cough test for a hernia. While it took only a few seconds, it was always dreadful. So when I had to go to the urologist for further examination and testing, I felt like all my male dignity had vanished like the viable sperm in my semen analysis.

Infertility seemed to confirm a truth grounded in a particular set of insecurities from my childhood. Simply put, I was not man enough. Though I was always big and tall for my age, I lacked the coordination to make those characteristics advantageous as an athlete. My uncle said that I "lacked heart." He meant I wasn't tough. I was soft. Even though our family boundaries were expansive and porous, we still had ways of creating wounds and causing harm. I kept those words and used them to nurse insecurity in my male body.

I wanted to be interested in sports, and I wanted to be good at them, mostly because I wanted to blend in with others. I wanted to be "normal." Still, I preferred music, reading, writing, and the arts in general. I was good at those things, and they felt natural even if they positioned me as abnormal in my social context. I would much rather spend hours practicing my instrument or reading than spend that time running drills over and over on field or court. The other boys thought this was crazy.

Even as my family had expansive notions of kinship and care, our notions of masculinity and manhood were not as capacious. Both of my parents had male siblings who received athletic scholarships for school and were scouted by professional sports teams. My dad was a star basketball player, and my older brother was too.

In the sixth grade, I begged my parents to let me play baseball, so they signed me up. On the first day of practice, I came home with a swollen eye. I was playing catcher and missed the catch with my glove but made contact with my eye. I was moved to center field—the position where I would do the least amount of damage. I think my prayer life was never as strong as when I was in center field, imploring, "Lord, please don't let a ball come this way. In Jesus's name, amen." Most of the time, my prayers were answered, but when they weren't, the opposing team was sure to score. Truthfully, I was just a horrible athlete, and my lack of skill in that area negatively impacted how I saw myself as a boy.

After a summer or two of sucking at baseball, I convinced my parents to let me go instead to finishing school, the only alternative summer program available at the time. At finishing school, I learned the "proper" way—the French way—to set a table and identify the number of courses of a meal by looking at the arrangement of the cutlery. I learned the importance of personal hygiene (I think this was the main reason my parents agreed to let me go) and three different ways to knot a tie. I learned how to escort debutantes at cotillions and formally introduce myself to dignitaries.

But all these skills made me a "sissy" to my friends. Petunia was not only one of my mother's favorite flowers but one of the nicknames given to me by my brother's friends. They called me this because while they were playing a pickup game of basketball or kill-a-man (an improvised version of football), I was helping my mom plant her garden.

So when I found out I was infertile, my mind went back to these childhood memories of a questionable masculinity and made a definitive judgment: you are still not a real man.

During this time, there were two men in my life, part of my Pennsylvania family, who I respected and cherished both as mentors and father/big-brother figures. One pastored the church I attended, and the other served as my field-education ministerial supervisor while I was in seminary. As much as I wanted to narrate my infertility as confirmation of an inferior masculinity, the presence of these men in my life would not allow it. Both of them were also infertile, unable to conceive children of their own, yet their lives as ministers and mentors told a different story about fruitfulness.

My pastor was in the process of training and encouraging a group of eight of us in the ministry, teaching us about preaching, leading worship, pastoral care, and church administration. My mentor was raising his two adopted sons while also planting a ministry and helping support campus ministers through fund-raising efforts. Both of these men had spent their lives pouring themselves into the lives of others and extending their networks of care and hospitality in ways that redefined fatherhood for me.

Infertility was not an indictment against my masculinity. It was an invitation for me to reconsider and reenvision how I would share my life with others. Neither my reproductive system nor my fears of not being man enough had to have the last word.

Fecundity

After sharing details about my infertility with a close friend who is a Roman Catholic priest, he said to me, "Nick, infertility does not rob you of fecundity. I am a priest, I have taken a vow of celibacy, I will never have my own biological children. But I am still a father—and not just in title, but in the way I am called to give my life in service to the church, in service to others. I very well may be biologically infertile. I will never know, but regardless, I am called to be fruitful and to nurture life."

I must admit, I had no clue what fecundity was when he said it. But after I looked it up, I could not shake the distinction he was pointing to between fertility and fecundity. The two words are often taken to be synonyms, but their particularity lies in their distinct roots.

Fertility comes from a word meaning "to bear." This idea of bearing is about productive capacity. To be fertile is to have the capacity to reproduce. *Fecundity* comes from a word that means "to suck or suckle, to nurse," thus affirming nurture as the substance of sustaining life. Being infertile is about my incapacity to reproduce life, while being fecund is about my capacity to nurse and nurture life. Fecundity is about my capacity to *make* family. While the ideal circumstance, as I understood it at the time, would have included both fertility and fecundity, the absence of one did not have to preclude the other. A focus on fecundity created a means for my wife and me to denormalize our understanding of the nuclear family and retrieve anew the values of "made" family.

We desired to be parents and knew that fostering and adoption would be our primary means to do so. We went through foster-parent training, and shortly after we finished, we took in two members of our extended family, my wife's cousin's kids. Our made family would emerge as a reconfiguration of blood relations.

The children lived with us off and on for about two years. It was a difficult arrangement, as we had no form of legal custody and were always at the mercy of the parents in caring for the kids. But we were committed to doing the best we could for them, in or out of our care. Eventually they were placed with their paternal grandmother, who is doing a fantastic job of caring for them.

But the experience was traumatizing in ways we still cannot reconcile. The arrangement kept us in a place of limbo, where we could not formally pursue fostering or adoption because we were caring for children who were not technically in our legal care. Nevertheless, we knew caring for the children mattered most, even if the arrangement was confusing and trying for us.

Just before my wife and I moved to Atlanta for my doctoral studies, we found out that her cousin was pregnant again, this time with twins. She was not in a position to care for the children in the way she wanted them to be cared for, so we stepped up again. We called the foster care office in DC and indicated that we were interested in kinship care. We wanted to take the babies into our home, and this is what our cousin wanted too. After we became licensed foster parents in Georgia, the twins were placed with us. A little over a year later, their adoption was finalized.

At the time of this writing, our boys are turning three. They have turned our lives around and provided a home for all our desires to love and care. They have reminded us that family is made by love and care. Through them, we know the power of love and the joy of care.

Not only has a focus on fecundity returned me to expansive notions of family, but it has also reformed my focus as a man. I am in a position to nurse my sons into expansive and diverse expressions of masculinity. As we are in the throes of potty training, I am recognizing daily the need to choose carefully my words about their bodies and how they do and do not use them. I do not want my sons to be ashamed of their bodies or feel that because their bodies work differently from others', they are somehow "less than."

My sons were born prematurely and were hospitalized for the first two months of their lives. Since they were nine months old, they have received physical therapy to help them integrate their sensory and motor systems. Like their dad, their hand-eye coordination ain't the best, but they love music and they love to dance. They are not born of my loins, but they are born of my heart and of my best substance. Who knows, maybe one day they will be skilled athletes, and that too will be a wonderful thing to celebrate. But if they can never throw a straight pitch or sing a perfect scale, they will know the power of love and the joy of care.

The gift of parenting is the gift of nurturing and tending. It is learning to extend care, to make space for care, and to make family through practices of care. My children do not understand what adoption is, but they know what family feels like. They do not understand what blood relations are, but they know the joy that comes from Auntie Jess's hugs and the laughter that comes from Uncle Julian's toss-ups. They know the routine of making Grandma's lunch in the morning before school. They know Grandma LoLo's garden in St. Louis and the satisfaction of her creamy oatmeal at the start of a day. They know love. They know family. They know the power of love and the joy of care.

To reimagine family as something more, or even other, than what we are born into is to recognize the way we make family, even as family makes us. For those of us who identify as Christian, this idea of a made family is essential to the Gospel. I like the idea of the realm of God and God's reign being about *kinship*, as opposed to *kingship*. Salvation as a means of kinship is about God's desire to make us a family through adoption. As Paul stated to the church at Corinth, not many of us are of noble birth, but God has called us. God has welcomed us in and made room for us.

The *kin*dom of God is fecund. The *kin*dom of God makes space for the stranger, the orphan, the widow, the outcast, and the forsaken. This inclusion is not about pity and narcissistic benevolence but instead about the true work of love in and through us. This inclusion bears witness to the Spirit's ability to transform us into agents of love and care.

We have been brought into the family of God through the fecundity of grace and the caress of faith. We now know the power of love and the joy of care. We did not have to earn our way or prove our worth. God's notion of family ruptures strict boundaries and makes room for whosoever will join. And when we are willing to extend the boundaries of our own families through radical forms of kinship such as fostering and adoption, both formally and informally, we live into the realm of God. Our homes and hearts as havens of sanctuary ensure that children know the power of love and the joy of care.

Reflection Questions

1 What practices encourage and foster openness and inclusion in my family?

2 How have I been included in others' families in ways that make me feel like kin?

3 What would it take for me to consider being a foster parent?

4 How can I widen the boundaries of family? Who can we name and claim?

5 How has my own experience of body and gender impacted my kids?

6 How do I need to shift my own habits, internal expectations, or understandings in order for my kids to feel alive in their bodies, loved in their families, and able to make their own borders welcoming?

2

Money

Nurturing a Family Culture of Generosity and Justice

Susan Taylor

Susan Taylor has spent her adult life in the intersections of justice and money. She is a partner at Just Money Advisors, which specializes in strategies that help investors work for justice through their finances. A PhD economist living in Louisville, Kentucky, Susan is the delighted and grateful mother of two young adults. She is the author of *What About Our Money? A Faith Response* (United Methodist Women, 2018) and resources for Faith and Money Network, where she is on the board. She also serves on the Mennonite Education Agency's Investment Committee and is on the board of Bartimaeus Cooperative Ministries.

Everyone's money story is different, based on their history, values, and emotions around money. This chapter brings together the stories of several families—across ages, geography, income brackets, and parenting stages—sharing their dreams and the practicalities of raising justice-rooted children in money-driven times. Some of the people interviewed are my friends, while others were referred to me as I sought a variety of life experiences among thoughtful, justice-focused parents. All of them shared generously and openly within the deeply personal territory that is related to money. Their stories are interwoven within my own experiences as a mother who creates justice with money professionally and what I have learned and unlearned about money while parenting my two children, now young adults.

The Challenge

All parenting is hard and joyous and befuddling and illuminating, but parenting around money can be especially challenging, because money comes with such a thick overlay of culture and emotion. Money is so pervasive in North American culture that it shapes some of the most critical aspects in our lives—what we eat, where we live, whether we have access to health care and education, and how we spend our days. The complex role of money is hard to grasp ourselves, much less teach our children.

We are told we need to plan for the future, but we don't know what the world will look like when our children are twenty or forty. We don't have a clue how much money they will need for education, health care, and housing—or to take care of us parents when we get old. The one thing I know my children will need later in life is this: models for living grounded in their values. Values around money will serve them no matter what financial stresses show up in their world.

Money is too often the root of injustice and the source of conflict. It is the foundation of an economy that doesn't work for most people or communities and certainly not for the planet. We can imagine an ideal economic system and work for those ideals. But as a parent, I can't wait until the systems are repaired or replaced. My children are here now, functioning in this economy. I want to prepare them to change the systems that exist but also to navigate the economy they are in. And that means learning to deal with money, including handling, saving, sharing, and spending it. It also includes understanding money in relationship to our own interests, personalities, values, and communities.

When economic systems within our homes are rooted in justice, we are teaching our children what they need to know to navigate money in a larger universe. And if we're paying attention, our children show us glimpses of that alternative economy we're looking for.

Unexpected Territory

I had anticipated that my children would have different personalities, but for some reason, I had never projected this in terms of the ways they would relate to money. At twenty-four and twenty-two, respectively, our daughter is extremely generous with her friends and generally enjoys things that cost money, while our son wants almost nothing that one would spend money on. These are the same traits we could see in them at ages six and four—Sara was treating her friends and playing with art projects and books, while Walker didn't even need props for his imaginary play.

This manifestation of the nature-nurture debate bends my mind. Celina Valera of Evanston, Illinois, shared by phone how she sees the same phenomenon in her children. Celina took her six- and seven-year-old children with her grocery shopping recently and allowed each child to buy one small thing. The older child bought a package of gum and was already on his third piece by the time they got to the car. The younger child selected gummies and climbed into the car saying, "I think I'll limit myself to two of these a day." Same parents, same money lessons, but different money personalities.

What a subversive statement: "I will limit myself . . ." A glimpse of the alternative economy.

Either personality can be both a blessing and a curse, depending on how it is applied. My daughter's generosity is sincere and lovely, but it makes it hard to keep money in her pocket. We have actively modeled restraints on consumption, for the sake of our hearts as well as the sake of the planet, but in a culture that says greed is a virtue, her generosity is a subversive act I try to learn from. My son's minimalism will serve him well in life, but those old pants won't cut it for a job interview. From him, I am reminded to keep asking myself, "How much is enough?"

Children's money personalities can stretch us as parents. Kate Foran and Steve Borla, from Hartford, Connecticut, describe themselves as anticapitalist introverts. So what is their older daughter's view of money? She is the consummate entrepreneur, of course.

"We have been thoughtful about parenting around money," Steve said, "but because of who she is, she's led us into territory we did not expect." At age five, their daughter Sylvia and a friend "had this idea to sell paper bookmarks in front of the house. Sylvia's friend lasted about ten minutes, but Sylvia was still going strong after several hours. She's continued to open her stand pretty regularly since then, and she's gone through a number of products. Pears from our pear tree. Flowers from our garden. She'll make fresh-squeezed lemonade if we've got the goods for it. She can sit out there for hours and loves interacting with people."

"I was horrified and embarrassed." Kate laughed. "We consider ourselves anticapitalists, and she's out there hawking her wares . . . [But] people are so receptive and supportive. People are happy to support a start-up human." As part of homeschooling, Kate enrolled Sylvia in a wilderness program celebrating the land's abundance, which has a practice called the "trade blanket," where natural items are exchanged. It exposes Sylvia to a different economic system, and according to Kate, Sylvia "works hard to make things for that" and "negotiates with her trade partners."

At age six, Gabe Hakim discovered the board game Monopoly in the rented cabin on a family trip. "It's a new fixture in our house," Gabe's father, Shady, said. "It has brought a lot of money conversations to the center." Erin, Gabe's mother, said, "He has a real interest in numbers: rolling the dice, counting the numbers, and acquiring. He likes to get things. And he likes exchanging. He doesn't mind paying, but he wants change back."

It's typical for children to love that exchange. Most young children think four quarters are worth way more than a ten-dollar bill, four being more than one. I once saw a photo of a dog bringing a leaf into an open-air store to exchange for a cookie, just like the people whom the dog must have observed. Paper money, a leaf—same thing to a dog. Children quickly move past that equivalence, but it takes time for developing, literal minds to understand the abstract nature of money.

Family Money History

I was extraordinarily lucky to have parents who were emotional adults. Growing up in the Great Depression understandably left many people deeply scarred and fearful, but somehow, my parents remained confident, open, and generous. My father taught high school in our midsize Kentucky town, and my mother taught at the local university, earning far more than my dad. Despite their professional status, their Depression-era skills stretched their incomes: they grew and canned our food, made our clothes and curtains, and did their own home repair.

They launched my brother and me with a college education and helped us financially when we faced crises or life transitions. As a young adult, I was serving breakfast one morning at a shelter, and a guest there told the story of how he became homeless. Speechless, I realized it was my own story—a stupid mistake of youth—with one key difference: my parents had helped me get my footing. I lived on little as a young adult, but never without backup, and that has made all the difference.

Nothing made my dad madder than greed. Growing up on a farm, he had seen neighbors lose their farms because they couldn't pay a twenty-dollar tax bill during the Depression. Many decades later, he sold his family's farm for a price well below market value to make it possible for a distant cousin to raise his own family on that land.

Every family has a money history. Our traits and emotions around money affect how we raise our children.

"I really do hate retail shopping, and shopping is such a big part of American behavior," said Dixcy Bosley-Smith of Washington, DC. "I feel like our kids have been blessed and victimized by our aversion to the traditional American consumerist lifestyle, in comparison to their peers. But they've grown accustomed to it." When her kids were little, Dixcy was told, "All you really need is a car seat, a jogger, and diapers." Dixcy thought, "What is it about society that we feel like we need a Home-Depot-sized baby depot?"

Like Dixcy, I hate to shop. While hugely pregnant, I fled in tears after my one trip to a baby superstore. How was I supposed to know which of the 123 different pacifiers my yet-unborn child would prefer?

My spouse, Andy Loving, and I talk about money way more than your average parents because we handle money for a living. We have a financial planning and investment management practice, specializing in helping our clients invest in the kinds of companies they want to support, as well as making their money available to people who traditionally are blocked from having access to capital—think renewable energy, organic farmland, fair-trade cooperatives, microcredit, and community banking.

When our children were young, we talked freely about social justice issues around money. They were convinced that fair-trade chocolate tasted better than "regular" chocolate and refused to shop at the big-box retailer, even if we couldn't find the kind of notebook required on their teacher's back-to-school shopping list anyplace else.

But it got stickier when we talked about our personal money. What are they ready to hear? What are we ready for them to repeat to their friends at school?! We told our kids when they were elementary school age that in a global context, we were quite wealthy. When the story was repeated at school, the global context was missing, and we became "really rich." And really embarrassed.

When it comes to money, silence rarely serves us. In my thousands of money conversations, I have observed that silence around money is the source of many personal money struggles, whether shame or pride, fear or fantasy, a sense of enough or never enough. In silence, children fill in the blanks, (mis)interpreting a parent's reaction to paying bills, for example, or imagining that they need to be responsible for the family's financial well-being. And silence around money serves the systems of injustice. To understand how money works in the world, framed by parents' values, prepares young people to see economic injustice and have the conviction and practical tools to respond in love and in power.

I was once sitting with a group of affluent adults who were beginning, at ages forty-plus, to question how much was enough for them. With a growing sense of how their lives, and lifestyles, were interconnected with people everywhere, both economically and ecologically, they wanted to respond in some way. Some in tears and some in resignation, most said they could not change a thing about the way they lived. They were trapped by mortgages, status, family expectations, or where their children were attending school—trapped by a lifetime of financial choices they had come to see as in conflict with what they wanted for themselves and for the world.

How much better off would our children be to understand money as young people, before they have accumulated a lifetime of financial baggage? If we teach our children about money early—if we offer them alternative models of living, if we teach them to question the assumptions our economy is based on and to challenge systems of injustice—perhaps we can help keep them free to respond to their deepest values and sense of purpose, as well as to their communities.

If we don't talk about money, our children's financial education will come from advertisers. And their peers.

Erin Hakim said Gabe came home from school one day saying, "I want a pair of shoes that has check marks on them." It took her a minute to understand that he was asking for Nikes. He eventually let it go, but he's a very socially driven person, according to his parents, and they wonder where that will lead regarding financial matters as Gabe grows up.

As kids get older, they see what other people have and "the different choices that different families make," Kate Foran said. "Sometimes Sylvia will say, 'When I'm an adult, I'm going to have a pool,'" or list all the things she wants. Kate remembers wanting things like that as a kid and tells her daughter, "When you're an adult, you can make different choices." Kate can see having strong values as both important and potentially a problem if "you push your kid away from your values because you're ideological about it." She added, "I can hope what she'll value, but she will have to come to this herself."

In school, my children learned little more about money than how to balance a checkbook—but they use debit cards and online banking, so that balancing-a-checkbook thing was about as useful as learning cursive. Despite all our family money conversations, my daughter wishes we had told her more about all the financial expectations she would face as an adult. She felt unprepared for how expensive life can be.

The information gaps were largely intentional on my part. I felt it would be overwhelming for a teenager to see all life's expenses before they have any sense of how they might earn income. I chose to introduce expenses more organically, one at a time as they arose. Feeling my way through, making judgment calls. I hear her critique, and I still think this was a reasonable decision for the personalities in our family.

Dixcy and Nolan made a different judgment call, showing their kids as teenagers where all the family money goes and sharing their tax returns. "We show them all the organizations we've given to every year and how that's connected to what we want to do in the world," Dixcy said. They also talk with their kids, as well as people outside the family, about aligning investments with their values. This level of transparency is not how either Dixcy or Nolan was raised, but it has served their family well.

Freedom to Be Generous

Parents with less money than they need have all these money issues to deal with in addition to the stress of not having enough. In the United States, we have cultivated a culture of shame around poverty. That is not true everywhere. Shannon Lockhart and her husband, Luis de Leon, lived for twelve years in a community of about 150 homes on the outskirts of Guatemala City. In Guatemala, she said, "a house is an investment, of course, but the real investment is in your neighbors." In the United States, we say that you can't pick your family, but in Guatemala, Shannon says, you can't pick your neighbors either, and the cultural expectation is that you treat them like family, because they are your family in community. They are your backup.

Though they loved life in Guatemala, the family was targeted for violence. Shannon and Luis moved to Louisville, Kentucky, with their sons (one of whom was then three, the other an infant) and have struggled to retain their community values here. "In Guatemala, we didn't pay for childcare," Shannon said. "We could borrow things, trade things. People look out for each other." Shannon described a "nonmonetary network" of people who give you the money you need for something, "assuming it's all going to work out" and you will help them in return when you have money to share. Loans are given without interest because interest is considered profiting from someone's trouble. It was a shock when they came to the United States, Shannon said. "Here, you have to pay for everything."

Shannon is a trauma therapist, working primarily with people without residency documents. Poverty is a key piece of both the struggle and the fear her clients live with. "A lot of their trauma is around money," Shannon noted. "They have medical debt or school debt. They are constantly harassed by debt collectors.

They paid so much to get here and now they have to pay for a lawyer to be able to stay."

Shannon refuses to add to their money worries: "I feel it's an obligation to use my values and skill set and faith to help." Consequently, her therapy practice runs on a pay-as-you-can system, meaning a significant portion of her clients pay little to nothing for her expertise and care. But other clients pay their own full fee plus more to cover someone else's care, something they wouldn't even think of at a standard doctor's office. "People are more generous when you allow them that freedom," Shannon said.

Luis works as a journalist for a Spanish-language news source in Louisville and is a musician in several bands. Both he and Shannon are visual artists as well. They serve their community broadly and creatively yet are paid little for their contributions. Shannon said her family is in debt and expects always to be in debt. "The system is designed for most people to never get out of debt, to never get ahead," she said. She and Luis align their fate with others by doing meaningful, community-building work, regardless of pay.

Now thirteen and ten, their children barely remember Guatemala, yet the community values their parents learned there have clearly been taught. The family lives across the street from a small park, and Luis said, "I can't think of how many times someone will be sitting in the park, and the boys run in saying there are people in the park who are cold or hungry. 'Make coffee, Papa,' they ask. Or, 'Make pancakes.'" Shannon shared, "We roll with it because that's what we taught them." She added, "It's not fiscally sound for this culture, but it's my obligation to share and not save for myself."

Caught, Not Taught

Like Shannon and Luis, all the parents I talked to said that a crucial aspect of communicating good money values, particularly for younger children, is more by modeling than words. As Nolan said, "It's caught, not taught."

"One of the things about parenting I imagined is that I would be imparting more wisdom," Kate admitted. "It doesn't really work like that. What is our family culture? What do I model? Me giving didactic lessons on these things doesn't work. [My daughter] is figuring it out."

As a child, Dixcy and Nolan's daughter, Colby Bosley-Smith, made signs and participated in vigils calling for financial divestment from private prisons. As a college student, she became part of the movement for her university to divest from fossil fuels, acting on those lessons learned.

A shared model across these families is hospitality. Erin said they frequently have friends staying in their home and "family is here constantly." Gabe sees an alternative that is sharply counter to the capitalist model of individualism and personal space. Celina and Peter Valera, with the support of their community, made the second floor of their communal home available to a high school senior who had no family care, giving him some security and the presence of caring adults as he finished high school. Shannon and Luis open their home to anyone who needs a meal and a place to stay.

A friend of Steve and Kate's lived with them the first couple years of Sylvia's life. When she was four, the family took in a man with a cognitive disability who had been wrongfully imprisoned for twenty years. "He had to have a family to be remanded to, and we signed up for that," Steve said. Nolan and Dixcy have had people emigrating from Haiti living in their home over the years and hosted several foreign exchange students for months at a time.

"Hospitality is easy when you're around Church of the Saviour," Nolan said, "because other people are doing the same thing." In Washington, DC, Church of the Saviour members routinely sacrifice time and resources to bring to life a large vision of Jesus's call for justice, building affordable housing, creating effective job and addiction recovery programs, offering nonpredatory financial services to low-income neighbors, and much more. Nolan said that at one point, he counted more than thirty households in his church community that had taken in refugees for months or years. "That's astonishing," Nolan remarked. "Growing up, our kids are going to church and seeing these people and are aware they are living with other folks. Being able to witness that at a level beyond [our household] is also important."

Celina and Peter Valera model a relational economy every day by living in intentional community. At Reba Place Fellowship, members' earned income is placed in a common purse, "and out of that, everyone's needs are met," Celina described. Each adult and child gets a set allowance, plus money for groceries—set as the state's food stamp allotment—and other household needs. Expenses for everything else, such as gas, medical care, or a vacation, are submitted to a small group for evaluation and reimbursement. "Our family lives off the same amount as another family," Celina said, "even if our work or pay is quite different."

Freely accepting limits set by others is truly a countercultural concept. Celina and Peter are careful and intentional about what they tell their children in this process, not wanting them to feel resentful. Rather than focusing on the limits, Celina said, "I talk about it more in terms of our ideals."

More Relationship, Less Stuff

Living in intentional community didn't feel like the right decision for our family, but that left us making all the decisions ourselves, which can be tough. I am not proud of some of the consumer/parenting decisions I made during periods of exhaustion, but we intentionally drew far more limits than my kids wanted at the time.

Almost twenty years ago, a group of friends and I started meeting for dinner now and then to share the stories of all the things we did that our kids thought were so mean: "I can't have a cell phone? You're so mean" (from a first grader), or "I can't hire a Hummer limo for my ninth birthday party like Julie did? You're so mean." Proudly, we dubbed ourselves the Mean Moms and continue to get together for a "rumble" now and then.

As a person who carries dreams for a just and peaceful world, I find that living in this transactional economy sometimes leaves me feeling wrung out and run over. Oh, how I wish my children lived in a relational economy instead.

We found pockets of that relational economy in our community. Some of our children's early friends were part of our small church community, being raised with values similar to ours—more relationship, less stuff, justice for all. What a help it was that some of their friends also had simple birthday parties and wore thrift-store clothes. Other friendships grew at their school, a public school that included students from every zip code in the county, ensuring not only racial integration but economic integration as well. There, too, we had amazing peers in parenting, people who contributed to and cheered for every child's successes.

We participated in a community meal group that shared two or three dinners a week. Those meals were precious time with beautiful people, a countercapitalism economy of shared food and open homes. Everything serves its time, and the meal group lasted well over a decade for us. But I can't help feeling that, at some level, the culture of individualism ultimately won. Meals became more complicated to cater to everyone's detailed dietary preferences, and kids' homework and extracurricular activities ruled family schedules and overwhelmed the priority of the community meals.

I wanted to protect my children from the toxic aspects of our culture—from exposure to sugar, fear, media, materialism—and to allow their hearts to define what is delicious and beautiful to them. To be rooted in values rather than valuables. It was easy to play defense, to make decisions to keep out certain aspects of consumerist culture. But I found it harder to make decisions around the things that were healthy and fun for them, such as activities and time with friends.

Are we willing to draw some limits around our kids to protect the community that is vital to our parenting? Reba Place Fellowship allows money for one lesson or team per child, supporting the community by setting some limits. When activities start pulling on the family and its finances, Dixcy and Nolan ask, "Is this something we have to do, or something we're getting sucked into?" What a useful, powerful question.

What does it mean to want what's best for our children? Do we move to a different neighborhood to get them into a particular school? Will their spirits be crushed if they don't get to attend their "dream college"? Do we have to make possible every opportunity that catches their eye? In what cases are we exercising our privilege with only an edge of shame because we are "doing it for our kids"?

Are we who have more than enough willing to actively redistribute from our surplus? Or go even deeper and redistribute from what we feel we need? Are we in community with people whose economic lives look different from ours, not as "helpers" and "receivers" but as cocreators of an economy with enough for all? An economy that lives within Earth's limits? An economy of justice, rooted in genuine peace?

No one knows all the answers to the questions that come our way as parents. I can't even know for sure when it comes to my own family, so I certainly can't speak for others. Nothing about money allows for purity. But with a clear sense of our values, the integrity to live from those values, and backup from our community, perhaps we can help our children find their role in creating the global economy of mutuality.

Reflection Questions

1. What is my family history around money, and how does it affect how our family relates to money today?

2. Who are people I can talk vulnerably with about money for accountability and encouragement?

3. How do I talk to my kids about money? What do I most want them to know? Am I modeling that for them?

4. What commitments that interact with money do I make toward justice? How do I include my children in the way I meet those commitments?

3
Education

Learning at the Speed of Trust

Kate Foran

Move at the speed of trust.

    —adrienne maree brown, *Emergent Strategy*

Kate Foran is from the woodlands of the
Connecticut River Watershed, where she
was formed by blue-collar poets, walkers,
fishermen, and Catholic Workers. She is a
freelance writer and poet from East Hartford,
Connecticut. She is a writing coach for Brave
Writer and serves on the board of Word and World:
A People's School. She is currently mentoring her
two daughters in self-directed learning.

---

*What would it look like if we could build a system of education that trusted
and respected children both for who they are now and for the productive
workers they may become? How do we educate knowing that we can't
"keep using the master's tools and expect to raise free people"? I wrestle
with these questions as I try to chart a path for my children's education.*

"There Is Nothing Wrong with Us"

One rainy June evening, I drove my nine-year-old daughter an hour from our home in central Connecticut to the shoreline city of New London. We would eventually stop to pay our respects to the ocean—past bedtime, with a storm coming in—but we came to see the performance-based presentation *Schools That Work for Us*. This show was the culmination of six years of research by Hearing Youth Voices, a youth-led social justice group working to transform the education system.

I made my daughter go—an example, perhaps, of where I bump up against the limits of my general "unschoolishness." But I want my white child, who has had little involvement with school so far, to practice centering the experiences of Black and Brown youth.

My reluctant companion soon understood that what she had expected to be a boring lecture was actually going to be a night of music, skits, and spoken word. The energy of the crowd was high, we ran into some friends, and there were even Wikki Stix at the welcome table to play with during the performance. We found a seat in the packed house and listened while young people took the stage to explore their framework for revolutionizing public schools.

"The system was not designed for us," the performance troupe of high school students declared. They continued,

> You may be asking, who's *us*? By *us* we mean—Black people, Brown people (non-Black Latino/Latinx, Asian, indigenous people); we mean poor people of all races;

we mean immigrants; people who speak languages other than English; we mean Black and Brown women; we mean queer or LGBTQ people; we mean disabled people.

If you look at any measure of student "success" that the Board of Education uses, or the State Department of Education uses, we are all behind. Test scores, graduation rates, college completion, attendance. Or we're ahead in the bad stuff—suspensions, expulsions, truancy. *What we're here to say to you today is that there is nothing wrong with us.* We are being asked to "succeed" in a system that was not designed for us to succeed.

The crowd cheered. Then the dozen or so youth on stage explored eight themes that constitute their framework for change, including the need for access to resources, the freedom to be and to move, support for mental health, and a sense of total safety at school. I got the sense that the preparation for this presentation was a better education for these kids than what they're offered in class.

Emergent Strategy

I've chosen not to enroll my kids in school for reasons that could fill a book. That decision is shot through with privilege. I have economic support from a partner, and I work from home. My privilege makes engaging in pure critique of school in this chapter feel boring and indulgent. Frankly, so does homeschooling my white children, sheltered from the issues that our neighbors face. Instead, I want to listen to brilliant youth and families who are claiming an education within the system or outside it.

So I sought out Chemay Morales-Brown, an equity consultant, former teacher, and current unschooler. She founded My Reflection Matters, a resource site and co-op for self-directed Black and Brown learners in Waterbury, Connecticut. The group includes her two young Afro-Latinx sons. She introduced me to the work of Akilah S. Richards, whose podcast, *Fare of the Free Child*, has the tagline "You can't keep using the master's tools and expect to raise free people." Both Chemay and Akilah see liberated learning outside of the system as resistance to white supremacy culture. They acknowledge how the school system ranks and compartmentalizes both knowledge and students, reflecting a hierarchical, fragmented, and abstracted worldview. They explore other, more holistic ways of interacting with reality that might be exactly what our groaning planet needs.

But knowing that the vast majority of kids still use school to get an education, I also looked to a few people who are committed to making public school work. I spoke with Laura Burfoot, the administrative director at Hearing Youth Voices (HYV). She is a white woman who, together with her wife, is raising their adopted teenage daughter, who is Black. I also talked to Maya Sheppard, a Black organizer for HYV and mom to a four-year-old boy. These two are not willing to cede the conversation about school over to charters, magnets, administration, teachers' unions, or any other interested party without hearing from students first.

I sat with Fatima Rojas, a Latinx mother and organizer in New Haven, Connecticut, who, among her many other community roles, cofounded New Haven Public School Advocates. Fatima is fiercely committed to public school as a right and responsibility. She recognizes the appeal of charter schools and other alternatives that prioritize play, movement, and restorative practices over standardized tests and discipline. But she has decided to keep agitating for her children's public schools to get the same benefits that the most cutting-edge, resource-rich white schools have.

The ideas of *emergent strategy* influenced my conversations with these folks. Emergent strategy stretches us to imagine a better future beyond dominant culture and its devotion to the commodification and control of people, land, and ideas. It challenges us to reconsider our human and more-than-human relations with the natural world and posits that "what to do" emerges from attending to those relationships. Principles include the following:

"Small is good, small is all": each interaction adds up, and the large is a reflection of the small.

"Less prep, more presence": listen to *what is* before imposing an agenda on it. Preparation has diminishing returns after a while, while presence has exponential returns. The sooner you move from preparing to being present, the better your results will be.

"Move at the speed of trust": How fast you can move is determined by how much trust you have. And people won't trust you unless you are vulnerable with them.

It's an approach relevant to everything from building community to helping a kid learn multiplication.

Through an emergent strategy lens, I explore how *trust* operates in education. What if we started with the premise that children *want* to learn? How do we move at the speed of trust in our relationships with learners themselves, their bodies, and their families? How does trust in children's resilience and trust in community allow for freedom and growth? These themes surfaced in my conversations with all the people I talked to, even though they sometimes had opposing perspectives on school.

Trust the Learner

Chemay Morales-James's organization My Reflection Matters (MRM) is a case study in how a person's needs and curiosities can guide the learning process. As she offered antiracist trainings, Chemay had a hard time finding resources for the classroom that reflected the experience of Black and Brown families. When she became a mom and looked for dark-skinned characters in books and on clothing for her kids, she could not find them: "It's like my sons didn't even exist." So she researched, connected with people, and found resources to create an online space where she could curate tools to support healthy racial identities.

Chemay is a former schoolteacher who enrolled her older son at age four in prekindergarten. The transition was hard for him. Chemay watched behind a two-way mirror for the first week, and she had never seen him so upset; he was crying and lashing out. She decided he wasn't ready and pulled him out. She figured they would try again when he was a little older. But she also knew that he was one of the few Black boys in the classroom, and in the back of her mind was her experience that "educators misperceive that behavior as belligerent."

Meanwhile, through conversations and research, Chemay discovered an approach to education that examines and critiques the coercive and emotionally and physically damaging habits often accepted as a normal part of adult-child relationships. She saw how we use power and manipulation to get kids on board with the school agenda. She began connecting with families who were experimenting with different ways of learning, and she noticed among homeschoolers of color a common feeling that "the system was not built for [them], and it's not set up to support [them]." She has heard similar feelings among white homeschool families of LGBTQ kids or kids with disabilities.

Chemay is interested in an approach to education that is not just about preparing a child to access the dominant culture's definition of success; rather, it's about freeing ourselves from what Todd Rose calls "the standardization covenant." Chemay explains, "It is realizing that we are in control of our own learning and don't have to rely on educational systems to define what our learning looks like." According to Chemay, "Equity is not the end. Liberation is what comes after equity. Liberation education for Black, Indigenous, and people of color (BIPOC) is about experiencing joy and exploring the gifts or treasures our ancestors left us and that often have been hidden from us."

This is an asset-based view of a person, a pedagogy of delight. Chemay said it took a long time for her to "deschool," or shift her fundamental ideas about education:

> Right now, my seven-year-old wants to fish all day . . . It's amazing what he learns. It requires a different kind of work for me than when I was a teacher. Instead of preparing tests and stressing about whether he's hitting grade-level targets, I . . . ask him at the start of the day, "What is your goal for the day?" . . . And he says he wants to compete in a fishing derby. What do I know about fishing derbies? So then I'm calling people with the skills he's looking for, especially as his learning outpaces my knowledge. I connect him with mentors. Sometimes I worry if he's hitting "grade level" or not. But then I ask, "What does that even mean? Who even made that up?"

Meanwhile, her son is pursuing goals and figuring out how to meet them and learning to read, write, and research by using those skills for his own purposes. At seven, he's motivated and self-actualizing. This educational approach has become a tool for organizing. Through MRM, Chemay now runs a liberated, self-directed cooperative that has grown to include some thirty-five Black and Brown youth. Children are part of MRM's decision-making. Some help facilitate classes, which include math, DJing, pottery, Bitsbox coding, and mala beading. Chemay and the other MRM families are reclaiming space in the generally white world of unschooling/homeschooling for the growing number of Black and Brown homeschoolers.

Paradigm Shift

Chemay gets some pushback, including from teacher friends who feel like she is undermining their profession. She knows the care and expertise teachers invest in their work. But she can only explain it as a paradigm shift.

I know that paradigm shift. I was an overly conscientious, nice white girl in a "good" (white) school system. I worked hard for school. I'm not sure it worked for me. Sure, I learned to read and write. But—at the risk of being flippant—since watching my daughter acquire these skills with little formal instruction, I'm not sure school should get much credit. Some evidence even suggests that children can learn all elementary math in under a year if instruction waits until after age twelve or so.

It's as though we push academics on young children because we as a society aren't quite sure what else to do with them. Meanwhile, I have spent most of my adulthood unlearning the lessons I absorbed in public school: be quiet, get good grades, make life easy for authority figures. Whatever spark of curiosity or intrinsic motivation I had survived in spite of this.

Like Chemay, my role with my kids involves caring for that spark. I'm not sure I fully claim "self-directed education"—the premise that a *self* exists in a vacuum outside of relationship seems like a symptom, maybe even a cause, of colonizer culture.

I have to be careful as a white person about raising another entitled white kid.

My kids' education emerges from their immediate needs in conversation with my broader perspective. Some skills require direct instruction, but close mentoring of an individual kid usually reveals when that approach is warranted. My kids' education arises from their interactions with streams and woods, Catholic Worker houses and demonstrations, books, classes, friends, projects, and play. We make the road by walking. It takes significant energy to respond to their interests and create a community and culture of learning that satisfies all our needs. Does this sound like a lavish use of resources? Sometimes I think so. I just can't shake the sense that every kid deserves mentoring like this.

In Chemay's view, if schools are to work for Black and Brown kids, we need culturally responsive and learner-directed pedagogy to become institutionalized in US education. She continues to work as an equity coach with schools, pushing for change. But for the sake of her own boys and the kids of the MRM network, she's not willing to wait. She sees homeschooling as the only liberatory option she has right now: "Hope hasn't died in me that there is a possibility of schools being transformed—but we almost have to tear the whole thing down and start from scratch. As a mom, I can't wait for that. Whoever wants to come along with me now, we can build together." She envisions a coworking space for self-directed learning with access to tools and resources—an art room, a kiln, a woodworking station. She wants to create an agile learning center that can also be used for after-school programs and as organizing space for activists and other groups focused on liberation.

Community Learning

Maya Sheppard, organizing director for Hearing Youth Voices, dealt with some of the same issues as Chemay when she enrolled her son in preschool. The only response his teacher had after the first few weeks of adjustment was "Your son is not complying, so we are collecting data on him." Maya narrates the thoughts that went through her head:

What does compliance even mean? Are you talking about the White model of compliance? Does he have any students or staff who look like him? How are you interacting with him? So I spend a lot of time in the classroom. I make sure his teachers see all of his caregivers as present: his dad, his grandmother, other community members. There are certain biases I encounter as a young Black woman. People assume I don't have any help and they're going to offer me services. They have no idea how much love I have poured into this child. My son is surrounded by love and care, and where that exists the least is in this classroom!

She recalls how these dynamics affected her own experience as a student: "I did not perform at expected levels. Now, at twenty-six, I realize I have a learning disability. But at the time people assumed I didn't care. I was met with all kinds of assumptions, an attitude of, 'I've dealt with students like you before.' But then I had an advisor who asked, 'What's going to work for you?' This teacher asked our whole class what we wanted. We felt ownership of the learning we did together. It solidified what a community learning experience can feel like. That's what I want to offer." Laura Burfoot says that HYV's pedagogy is rooted in this kind of community learning experience. In the tradition of popular education, youth participate in crafting the organization's agenda. Says Laura,

> We are about getting young people in the room to think about and name where they do have power, and where they do not. We want them to experience people power and to practice agitation, to "fight back." In terms of leadership development, what we've done well is we've built a culture where it's okay to make mistakes. We organized a forum for board of education candidates, and the youngest person, new to the group, wanted to be the emcee. So do we try to control and protect? Or do we say, "Okay! You trust yourself to be the emcee! Go for it." We say, "Go for it." Sometimes that leads to pretty big mistakes. But we deal with mistakes together. The process is messy. But so much learning happens in that process.

Get it done indeed: HYV recently helped push for legislation in Connecticut requiring a Black/Latinx history class to be offered in every high school across the state. Students testified, advocated, and decided where to compromise. The legislation passed. It was a big win and a learning experience. I've noticed from watching my own children that they crave real work. How much more powerful is it to prepare a presentation for state legislators than to write a report for social studies class?

Maya says this approach can work for any area of learning. Kids who struggle can feel anxious, pressured, or ashamed and will find a way to resist. Instead of interpreting their resistance as willfulness or laziness and punishing it, she says, we need to give them the benefit of the doubt and find out what's behind their behavior. This point is especially true for BIPOC kids who are systematically and violently denied the benefit of the doubt.

Freedom to Move

Children learn through their bodies, not just their minds. And bodies need to move. One of the themes HYV students are advocating for is the "Freedom to Be and to Move." They write, "It is not a coincidence that the schools like ours that have the most restrictive and high-control environments have majority Black and Brown students. We live in a country that monitors and restricts Black and Brown people, everywhere and at all times."

For Fatima Rojas, freedom to move means respecting how kids need to inhabit their bodies—and not just during recess. "The length of the school day, the amount of time they spend sitting—it's not developmentally appropriate," she says. She shared videos of kids jumping during math class to practice numerators and denominators and a clip of kids moving around outside in the school courtyard during science class—both the result of Fatima's advocacy.

Fatima visited her daughter during lunch one day and witnessed the chaos of an elementary lunchroom: teachers with the nearly impossible job of managing a room full of energetic eleven-year-olds, yelling into a microphone, insisting that children put their heads down when they were finished eating. When the principal defended the practice of requiring heads down, Fatima insisted, "When rules are not serving human dignity, you need to change them. I said to the principal, 'You are Taino and I am descended from the Aztecs, and that's what the Spaniards did to us: they told us to put our heads down. And we were supposed to say, "Yes master." No more.'" The practice is now banned at the school.

Fatima's kids attend a dual English-Spanish language Comer school, based on a holistic strategy linking children's academic, emotional, moral, and social growth. According to Fatima, even though the school is set up on a consensus model, parents must push for inclusion. She recalls chaperoning a prekindergarten field trip for her younger daughter to a local orchard.

Fatima left work to chaperone. As she approached the school through a drizzle, other parents informed her, "We are not going to pick apples because of the weather. It's too dangerous." When Fatima confronted the teachers, they told her something about liability. Fatima, a native Spanish speaker, asked what "liability" was, and when the teacher couldn't explain, she looked it up on her phone. Then she declared, "Let's go pick apples."

Fatima pushed against the unilateral decision and this institutionalized lack of trust between the system and the people it's supposed to serve. As she says, "Is not the rain a part of knowledge? Is not the change of matter—when water mixes with dirt to make mud—is that not science?" She made rain ponchos out of bags, and the kids had a blast.

So began a partnership with another parent chaperone to start New Haven Public School Advocates, which represents forty-six schools and twenty-two thousand students and aims to monitor, document, analyze, and publicize decisions that affect the education of students in New Haven public schools to shine light on meetings and other processes that, while technically public, are sometimes difficult to access. In Fatima's community, fear of deportation keeps some families out of schools, which is why Fatima continues to advocate for New Haven's sanctuary city status to make it safe for undocumented families to be involved in their kids' education.

Resilience

Part of trusting kids is offering confidence in their ability to face challenges. Fatima's older daughter confronted a substitute teacher who threatened to take away recess for unfinished worksheets. Fatima's daughter raised her hand and respectfully advocated for herself and her classmates: "You can't take away recess; that's illegal." The teacher only backed down after Fatima's daughter asked to call her mom. To be fair, teachers are often in an impossible bind, pressured to cover the material required. But Fatima says, "I believe that kids can defend themselves, especially if parents teach them their rights."

Laura says of her daughter's education in a majority-Black public high school with mostly white teachers,

She's learned a lot of lessons, like how to stand up and call out teachers who are being racist, classist, sexist. I want to raise a kid who knows how to stand up like that, who knows how to assess whether she has enough stamina, and if the answer is yes, then to do it. If the answer is no, then save your energy, come home, and we'll hold you and figure out whether to fight together or let it go. I'm not big on sheltering. I'd rather raise a kid to go out in the world and experience the shit but to have enough of a safe place at home to process it.

Do I think she's getting the best literacy experience or academics in the world? No. But is she brilliant, figuring out how to fight for herself and for others, take a stand, even if it's hard and scary? Yes, she's learning how to do all that.

And I ask myself, who are the humans we need right now in this moment? We need ones who are experienced at taking a stand. Because as I see it, until we end White supremacy and capitalism, there are no good schooling options for Black and Brown youth.

This position challenges me to my core. In opting to keep my kids out of the school system, I know that I am exercising my *choice*, the buzzword of school reform at the moment. But in the context of rampant consumerism and inequality, *choice* is suspect. *Choice* is an overlay on a system that trades people's time, freedom, health, and the health of the planet for a few more cereal options at the grocery store. *Choice* is a joke for most marginalized families.

Still, education at the speed of trust might be an "experiment in truth" in the face of a hegemonic system that serves an unjust economic order and that serves its own perpetuation, as institutions do, over the needs of people. We need people pushing the system from within, above, below, and outside—the same way we need people working the radical edges of New Afrikan economics and off-the-grid ecovillages and antinuclear actions while others are running for office or taking socially responsible investing as far as it will go. I think we need, as the Zapatistas say, "a world where many worlds fit."

But Laura is clear that Hearing Youth Voices is working for a world that has never existed. The organization hosts a spectrum of opinions as to whether they should be influencing dominating institutions or building their own. Since acknowledging that they are doing both, there's much less infighting! But they are not backing down from a broad, ambitious vision: "What we want is a *publicly funded and supported* education system that allows for true freedom and self-determination no matter what, for Black people, Brown people, poor people. Actual true freedom and self-determination—that's what we've never had. We've had Black schools for Black people about true freedom and self-determination during and after Reconstruction. But they weren't resourced by the state; they weren't invested in by all of us, with our taxes, the way white schools were. So how do we build the political will for that? I don't have the answer."

God knows I don't have it either. But I know we need people doing the work on all fronts the way Laura and Maya and Fatima and Chemay are doing it. I intend to show up for their efforts. They are fighting for all our kids.

* * *

Meanwhile, other ways of knowing call to me, along with other ways of being with children—integrated into the life of the community rather than separated from it. Images of child-sized handprints and carvings on prehistoric cave walls dance around the knowledge that *we must live our next civilization now*. Sometimes poems can explore these ideas in ways essays can't . . .

Ancient Futures
"Maybe it's like this past couple of centuries is just a blip and
    humans are about to go back to normal." —a friend, on
    climate catastrophe
One daughter learns to count on her fingers, her tiny nails like
    shells,
polish chipping off, thumb pinning pointer down to hold up *three*.
The older girl, farther along, holds an equation on her digits
    while she ciphers.
Base ten built into these bodies, the original manipulatives.
Watching a child develop is like watching human evolution on
    a small scale;
the growth of infant brains mirrors the differences
between other primates and humans.
You can witness abstractions like *numbers* or *the past*
dawn on them and catch like flint sparks.
At the Cave of a Hundred Mammoths, archaeologists find
    child-art,
finger flutings carved in soft clay on the cave walls, some on
    the ceiling.

Someone tall lifted someone smaller and waited while the
  child
marked lines and shapes to her perfect satisfaction.
There are no areas in Rouffignac with flutings
where we find adults without children, and vice versa.
Origins seem important, so I read the kids a tale about
how the need to count might have emerged among early
  herders.
Amu did not think of his herd as "nine" sheep.
He thought of the herd as all his fingers but one . . .
Prehistory is a kind of speculative fiction.
So is the act of educating a child.
Their time with me is on loan from an unknown future.
Curiosity is gratitude, I tell my older girl,
Learning is a way of loving the world.
What will they need to know when they grow up?
Will their nails collect dirt digging for roots to eat?
I signed one up for coding class.
Math is a way of using what you know
to figure out what you don't know, I tell her.
She works on a problem, grasping it in her mind.

She practices borrowing and carrying.

Reflection Questions

1 How do I square a system of compulsory schooling with values of liberation?

2 How do I build political will for publicly funded communities of learning that support freedom and self-determination for all kids, especially BIPOC kids?

3 How does my social location impact my decisions around education?

4
Where to Live

Putting Down Roots and Being Known

Frida Berrigan

Frida Berrigan lives in New London, Connecticut, with her husband and three children. A war-tax resister, community gardener, and writer, Frida contributes to TomDispatch and Waging Nonviolence. She is the author of *It Runs in the Family: On Being Raised by Radicals and Growing Into Rebellious Motherhood* (OR Books, 2015), which recounts her experience growing up at Jonah House, the community founded by her parents, Elizabeth McAlister and Philip Berrigan.

Where is our home? How long have we been there? Do we know our neighbors? This essay is about how I learned to value home and rootedness and am now cultivating that for—and with—my children. We are living in a time when there is a sort of privilege of placelessness. One can be at home anywhere connected to comfort and convenience. Uber, DoorDash, and Amazon mean that you can meet your needs without human connection. But what do we need more than human connection, really? I am reflecting on the boon and benefits of rooted stewardship as a sort of antidote to the fluidity of modernity. I wrote all this before COVID-19 fixed us firmly in whatever place we were, rooting us all whether we liked it or not! But a few months into a new way of being, I am grateful for a home-place, a sense of self in relationship to a wider community, a web of resistance and restoration that is anchoring amid the waves of pandemic worry—and political terror—that crash over me.

Our Neighbors Know When the Tomatoes Are Ripe

My daughter and I grow strawberries in our front yard. It is a weedy little patch, and finding the strawberries takes work, but it is worth it. The berries are red and sweet, wet from the morning dew, warm from the sun, and best eaten in that very moment. We share with the kids waiting for the bus.

Our garden slowly expands each year: tomatoes, beans, basil, collards, and a few stalks of popping corn. We have squash plants growing out of the compost bin and blueberries that we share with the birds. We planted a plum tree and two apple trees—and a grapevine a few years back that struggles amid the weeds.

We live in an old whaling town along the Connecticut coastline, where the Thames River meets Long Island Sound. New London is halfway between New York and Boston and halfway between New Haven and Providence. It is a place where place matters, where saying the name of your street discloses your class and position. The old guard holds on hard here, but change is coming. The complexion, cadence, and color of our town are changing. It is beautiful and dilapidated, struggling amid the weeds too.

Our neighbors know when our tomatoes are ripe, and we share the providential bounty in a rainbow of orange, red, yellow, and a color so purple, it's almost black. Our fig tree teaches us about resurrection every year. I love this garden, this tiny patch of earth. It is fecund, surprising, in constant need of care and attention. This is my home, on a busy street in a small town. I love New London too. In this small town, I feel visible, accountable, and known. I am finding rootedness.

All this rootedness, all this fecund front yard growth, didn't just happen. It was a decision. And it might be the most radical act of my forty-six years: to know where I stand and to stand there under the rainbow peace flag that snaps from our flagpole.

When I was growing up, we didn't grow much besides a handful of flowers. Our yard was small and utilitarian. It was mostly taken up by a woodpile of downed telephone poles soaked in creosote and limbs scrounged from parks after storms. My dad would bring the ax down on the rounds, and his suspenders would snap as the head buried in the dense wood. My brother and I helped, transferring the chunks of wood to the pile in too-big gloves that got our fingernails dirty and smelled like car oil. Rats loved nesting in our woodpile, and so we'd have to dismantle the whole thing every once in a while to wage war on them.

We heated our narrow, four-story row house with this wood. And it was one of my chores to bring loads to the stoves. People came from all over to live at Jonah House—the name my parents and their friends gave to the house when they started renting it in 1973. Sometimes it was full. And that meant hauling wood all the way up to the third-floor front room, where three people lived; then to the second-floor room, which two people shared; then to the main floor, where the dining room and living room were; and finally—easiest of all—to the stove that heated our family's rooms in the basement. People who came to learn about nonviolent resistance, Christian simplicity, and Gospel witness with my parents and the community also got to enjoy the wood-burnt warmth and the scent of Baltimore's bounty of scrounged firewood.

Once the wood baskets on all the floors were full, the job still wasn't finished. I had to sweep up all the dirt and wood chips I had tracked in from the many trips in and out, up and down. Only then was I was done, with no need for a fire, because I was hot and sweaty.

If we wanted flowers for the house church altar, Dad and I would go out into the neighborhood in the early morning with his pocketknife and carve off blooms from the yards of our greener-thumbed, more well-heeled neighbors. One man always seemed to be looking out his window, and he would yell at us and curse us for picking his flowers. Dad thought it was funny. He'd laugh and yell back that flowers aren't property. I look back now and feel protective of that man and his hard-earned urban beauty. My own sidewalk flowers suffer from the attention of passersby. And while I wouldn't yell at a kid, I notice when the buds I've been watching open bit by bit end up crumpled at the end of the block.

Provisional Relationships

My parents never voted. My father would say, "If voting mattered, it would be illegal." The glib line holds a deeper wisdom about how it was illegal for many people to vote and how the franchise is still under assault where it matters most. As far as I know, my family members didn't involve themselves in city politics. They didn't go to city council meetings or join the neighborhood association.

Our community was off the grid and noncompliant in every sense. We were rooted in a way of life, not a location. We were ascetic, spare, and unsentimental. All that made it seem like we floated a few inches above the daily concerns of our neighbors. We lived in solidarity, which means we were actually sharing in the lot of those around us, but I didn't see that then.

Our homeowning neighbors hated that we gave away food on the corner early every Tuesday morning, sharing what we had obtained from dumpster-diving at the local produce terminal. Our renting neighbors collected these anarchist gleanings and knocked on our door when they needed twenty dollars to carry them to the end of the month. We were renters too. We aligned ourselves with the transient, poorer, Blacker majority of our neighborhood instead of with the white homeowners and their carefully tended flowers.

My parents didn't own anything: not the tall, thin house at 1933 Park Avenue in Baltimore, not any of the cars we drove, not a personal bank account. The Jonah House account held the money they earned painting houses and donations from friends and supporters. It did not belong to my parents. They didn't want to be owners. Property is theft, after all. And beyond principle, it was easier to be war-tax resisters if you were poor and didn't have anything worth seizing.

The neighborhood I grew up in was called Reservoir Hill. At a conference a while back, I met a young white woman who teaches at a Catholic school in Baltimore. We played the neighborhood game, even though I knew how it would end. "Ooh," she said, "it's rough over there now. Was it good when you lived there?"

Yes, it was good. It was real. It was poor and Black and underserved, but we had friends. We played ball in a trash-filled lot and threw Osage oranges at each other. We swam in the park fountain near the "No Swimming" signs—even after I cut my foot badly on submerged broken glass.

It was good. It was rough. After I went away to college, the city knocked down a whole section of Reservoir Hill—blocks and blocks of houses that had once been homes—as a way of "redeveloping" the people out of their neighborhood.

It was good. It was awkward. In elementary school, my brother and I were the only white kids. We were pudgy, freckled, and uncomfortable in our secondhand politics and outfits. We had half-adult views adopted from the passionate, verbose grown-ups around us who talked national and international politics all the time.

All our T-shirts bore political slogans. In fourth grade I wore a red T-shirt with a black drawing of Emma Goldman and the message "If I can't dance, I don't want to be part of your revolution." Embarrassed in my own skin, I wouldn't have danced for all the sharp-collared polo shirts in the world, but it was my favorite T-shirt.

My family's provisional relationship to property and local politics rubbed off on me. In high school, I knew more about what was going on in Bosnia-Herzegovina than in my own city—even though Baltimore was as balkanized and full of hidden fault lines as that ravaged former Soviet state and burdened by the sickness of white supremacy too.

"Know Where You Stand"

When I was in college, my community left our home without sentiment or nostalgia. Most of our furniture—third-hand and mismatched but full of memory—was also full of roach eggs and was left behind. My parents and the rest of the community did not look back. They became the caretakers of an Irish Catholic cemetery with lots of land for gardens and fruit trees. I helped with the transition a little, but I mostly missed it. One day I came home from college to visit and their home was in a new place.

But it wasn't my home. My childhood home, so crowded with object-free memories, is now someone else's house. I've passed by, but the huge front window, once crowded with plants and political messages, is covered with substantial venetian blinds and devoid of personality. Somewhere inside that house is a repaired wall that once bore the outline of my brother's bulk. We were fighting in the hallway, and I pushed him hard. He fell into the wall, and the aging plaster gave way and was imprinted with his outline. We hid the damage behind a tapestry—for a while anyway.

As a young adult in Brooklyn, I was a serial renter. I hovered above the surface of my location. I never saw the point of getting to know my neighbors. I loved them, but I did not want to pause for them. I performed my activism in Manhattan, in public, in spectacle, and then I went home to expensive apartments in poor neighborhoods. I knew that the big issues I was activated by—the global war on terror, Islamophobia, mass incarceration, and inequality—all had hyperlocal analogs and manifestations. But I wanted to make a difference, and to me at that time, making a difference meant marching in Manhattan. So I went off to my meetings and marches and drank the four-dollar coffees from the cute shops that started sprouting up in my neighborhood and bought thirty-dollar bottles of wine from the adorable almost-all-organic wine store and marveled at how, all of a sudden, people my age were buying million-dollar fixer-uppers on my block.

This was a posture I could have sustained for a while. Someone was always asking: Are you going to Seattle? Are you headed to Cindy Sheehan's encampment? Are you going down to School of the Americas? There was always someplace to go: encampment, mobilization, occupation to support with my time and body and money.

Go go go go go go. Go where? Go why? Dan Berrigan said, "Know where you stand and stand there." It took me a while to hear my uncle's advice. But I finally listened. After all those years bopping around Brooklyn, then a stint in a tiny room at Mary House Catholic Worker, I was ready for a change. I was ready for rootedness—a kind of unchangeable change.

Four-Walled Freedom

"I was enclosed in the four walls of my new freedom." That is how Thomas Merton described arriving at the Abbey of Gethsemani in December 1941. He was leaving the modern world to become a contemplative monk. To our modern ears, freedom is defined as the exact opposite of four walls—particularly the Gothic masonry walls of a monastery. Freedom is impulse, frivolity, a life without consequences or responsibilities.

Living at the corner of Cedar Grove and Connecticut Avenue, roused by the deep bass of passing cars and the grinding vibration of crotch rockets, I connect with Thomas Merton's freedom. Home is made up of so much more than four walls—and yet you need those four walls to hold it up. Bound by four walls built in 1921, plastered today with our pictures and posters, I now bear the small-town obligation of politeness and the street nod, the duty to know one's neighbors and account for the state of my lawn. Our neighbor Dave calls our overgrown yard Sherwood Forest and makes a very definite line with his lawn mower where our properties meet.

The four walls of freedom give us a place to stand. They give us a vantage point from which to look forward into an uncertain future and to see ourselves there, to see our children there, to be able to build on the network of relationships in our neighborhood to take care of one another. Our children will learn by our example. Somehow our future adults will (we hope) be compassionate, skilled members of a resilient community. It is hard to see sharing tomatoes out of our front yard as a lesson in cultivating an urban agrarianism built in the shell of Trumpian capitalism's collapse. But we gotta get there somehow.

From this place of standing, we are also able to look back, learning the bloody, brutal, very profitable histories of whale hunting and slave trading that built the early beauty of our town. We can tell the story of Adam Jackson, an enslaved man who lived five blocks from where we stand, under the control of a man named Joseph Hempstead. Hempstead kept a diary, and from that record—and the book *For Adam's Sake: A Family Saga in Colonial New England*—we can know bits and pieces of Jackson's life. The pieces that we know challenge the assertion that Northern slavery was genteel or gentle. And all that is not just a history lesson but a daily stance for today that seeks reparations, builds right relationships, and searches for the hard answers.

From these four walls, we are free to go even further back, to the year 1637 a few miles up our coastline. On May 26 of that year, Connecticut colonists attacked a Pequot village surrounded by a high palisade with only two exits. Hundreds of men, women, and children were asleep in a cluster of small houses within. The attackers set the village on fire, blocked the exits, and shot anyone who made it over the wall. Between four hundred and seven hundred people were killed. And we were there, in the form of a great-great (plus twelve or thirteen?) grandfather of my husband and children named Nicholas Olmstead. In his report of the raid, the general in charge called Olmstead out in particular, praising him as one of the two brave men who crept into the village to set the fire. And we are still here, in the form of current beneficiaries of white supremacy.

It is a responsibility of rootedness to weave that horror and history into the warp and weft of our lives. And so we walked with the monks and nuns of the Leverett Peace Pagoda, connecting and uncovering the sites of colonial massacres. And our children walked, meeting elders of different communities in Connecticut and Massachusetts, hearing stories and learning that showing up is the first step to understanding connection and responsibility and building compassion and solidarity.

This connection to the past also brings joy. My mother-in-law gave my son a T-shirt for his seventh birthday. My husband, Patrick, had tie-dyed it at a playgroup when he was six or seven and wore it to a faded shine. Seamus wears it now, some thirty years later, and I revel in that object-based memorialism. And I feel a pang of loss for my own childhood objects that held no narrative magic for my pragmatic, forward-looking parents They honed their own needs to a narrow point and taught us to be as pared down and unsentimental as they were.

We are teaching rootedness to our active, distractible children. In the way we talk about the land and our community. In the way we help them pick up trash along the streets. In the way we encourage them to greet adults and know our neighbors' names. They come with us to city council meetings and board of education meetings. They've met the mayor and are always happy to see our state representative, Anthony Nolan (who has a big dog they love), and our city councillor, Alma Nartatez (who, come to think of it, also has a very friendly, lovable dog). They listen to us talk about local politics and want to participate along with us.

And they work in the garden, they share strawberries with their friends, they correct people when they litter. It all starts here. And here we are. Planted. Rooted in new soil and reaching down, growing up, branching out.

Reflection Questions

1 Am I *from* a place? How do I benefit from a sense of place? Do I benefit? If not, why not?

2 Does place identity mean something to my children? Do I learn anything from their rootedness?

3 Some of us can "feel at home" anywhere. Is that a good thing? Where is privilege in that unrooted sense of place?

5
Spirituality

Entrusting Our Children to the Path

Dee Dee Risher

Dee Dee Risher is a writer, editor, and retreat leader. She is the author of *The Soulmaking Room* (Upper Room Books, 2016). She was editor of the Christian social justice magazines *The Other Side* and *Conspire*. She is a cofounder of Philadelphia's Alternative Seminary and helped start Vine and Fig Tree, a faith-based, intentional cooperative housing community in the Germantown neighborhood, of which she is a longtime resident. She has published more than two hundred articles in such magazines as *Sojourners*, *Progressive Christian*, the *Utne Reader*, *Geez*, and *Grid*, and her blogs appear in the *Huffington Post*, *Theological Curves*, and other venues. She and partner William O'Brien are grateful for all the things their children Luke and Thea teach them.

These musings reflect on how my partner, Will, and I tried to nurture our children's innate sense of spirituality—how we offered them a framework of meaning. Our children are now nineteen and twenty-one, and who knows what fruit our intentions have borne—or will bear in the future. I believe that parents should intentionally explore with their children the deep spiritual roots of being human. What tradition and what shape that takes will be as varied as we are as parents. The journey has no right answer. Instead, it is about raising the questions and living toward a path that carries us to meaning.

A Different Kind of Love

Within a month of my first child's entry into the world, I knew that I had birthed a life that would challenge my own spiritual journey to the core. Raising my two children arose in me tumultuous emotions, conflicts, and endless spiritual gifts. My journey as a parent brought to the surface deep and critical spiritual work I needed to do.

Yet even as my children gave me a bunch of spiritual issues to work on over the years, it was also clear from the outset that I had to assume some kind of spiritual-director role for them. The historical moment in which they were born was full of greed, violence, hatred, selfishness, and the looming threat of climate change and environmental collapse. In such a time, they would need their deepest grounding to navigate and resist. They would need faith, resilience, and a deep spiritual path to carry them in an era in which the single constant is rapid change.

In those first months after my son's birth, I was drenched in the two primal lessons of healthy parenting: unimaginable love and endless self-sacrifice for that love. Under the unending blur of bodily functions and the relentless craving for sleep that launch parenting lies a stark truth: our parents love us more than we love them.

I loved my parents, certainly, and had always viewed that love as reciprocated in about the same strength. But suddenly I was glimpsing it from the inside, as it must have been at the beginning, inscrutable and a mystery beyond words. The love we have for our children is not love we can give back to our parents in the same fierce intensity. Every generation pours out love to the next. However flawed and human and broken we may experience our parents (for we are all flawed parents), they carry for us a different kind of love from that which we return to them. Certainly trauma, abuse, and evil can distort this parent-child cycle and even extract all love from it. But in healthy situations, a parent is overwhelmed with the desire to care for and protect their child and gives endlessly to do so.

A Revelatory Path

My partner, Will, and I have always found our grounding in the Christian tradition. We wanted to teach that to our children, not because this was a dictated path to their salvation but rather because, for us, this path has been a revelatory way to live in the world. It has been for us a path toward love, carrying us into redemption, resistance, and transformation. It is a spiritual corrective for basic human tendencies toward selfishness, violence, and ego-centered living. I believe that the more specifically we ground ourselves in our religious and spiritual traditions, the more we are able to speak across them.

Many parents who come from a Christian background believe that giving our children a spiritual rearing consists of finding the right church/faith community, complete with a good children's program, and signing up—kind of like finding the right preschool. Usually, we look for communities that reflect our values. We volunteer as Sunday school teachers or serve on the education committee, and we get our kids to church. My children, now in their late teens, would be the first to say that our different church communities have been extremely formative in cultivating their faith, spiritual resilience, and commitments to justice. I believe that investing in a faith community is a very important choice to make.

But we cannot cede the task of guiding our children's spiritual development to a religious community and wash our hands of it. Our spiritual rearing of our children begins much sooner, in those early months. This is when we fall in love with our children and truly learn to love them unconditionally. Ahead are the parental challenges that will involve conditions, consequences, punishments, judgments, and tricky emotional terrain, but in this first season, they are what they are, and we try to comfort them and provide for their needs.

The spiritual needs of infants and small children are not complicated but nonetheless can be hard to deliver. First, they need security and a sense of safety. They need to feel love in the tangible ways of human touch and voice, eye and hand. Yet it is also a time to be spiritually aware: wise as serpents. As a parent with privilege (skin color, economic security, education), I sensed immediately how easily I could lose myself to the principality of privilege, always unconsciously putting my children ahead. I could be fully absorbed in giving them the best access to everything I could afford.

It feels so selfless to pour out all we have on this being we love. That quickly can become buying the best house, education, neighborhood, and family adventures we can. We do so unconsciously, or we rationalize using the many systems of privilege we are able to access on behalf of our own. For those of us with some privilege, it is a fine balance to live out: What do our children need, at a core level, and what should we not offer them, even if we can, because we want to live toward a wider justice? What choices must I forgo for my children because I don't want to buttress a system that rewards unevenly and instead want my choices to widen access so that more children can share in what is now a privilege?

What is the spiritual fruit when we use our economic privilege to offer our children "the best" in schools, neighborhoods, clothes, and goods? I cannot say it is ultimately destructive, or that children raised this way wreak havoc. On the contrary, often these children become very well-educated forces to set the world right. What haunts me, rather, is Audre Lorde's insight: "The master's tools will never dismantle the master's house." Parents of privilege (like me) who are not willing to deny their children certain avenues of privilege will never be able to dream or construct a more equitable world in which privilege is abandoned and the playing field is leveled. This must be our ultimate goal, because any spirituality I believe in has to center on love, justice ("what love looks like in public," Cornel West says), and the creation of community.

Life as Miracle

What do children need for healthy spiritual development? Every parent will answer that differently, according to what they value. I realized that it was very important to me to expose my children daily to the impossible immensity and beauty of the natural world. Even though we live in a dense, low-income urban neighborhood, I wanted them to see, very early on, the unspeakable wonder of other life-forms: plant, animal, mineral. I wanted them to realize that they were a part of the fabric of creation—a weave in the cloth, not the dominating master of the universe.

Life is a miracle, and no one is more attentive and squanders more time on watching it than children. Even if our lives are concrete-bound, nature is everywhere: the insect kingdom is immense and pervasive, the sky swimming with expressions and color, the vegetables in your kitchen lovely, and there are trees and parks near. In a consumer world in which children see every adult with a minute of spare time pull out and scroll a phone, offer them this other attention. Give them the world that holds us instead of the fabricated world that distracts us, and you will discover that you have given it to yourself. Should this planet survive human habitation, it will be because our children learned to care again, relentlessly and more deeply, for the earth.

Beyond that, it was important to me to give them family—as diverse as we could. I wanted to give them people and conversation and relationship. We limited any usage of devices around people. We had lots of people over for dinner, and conversation was always rich and varied. Now that our children are in the older, almost adult years, this principle has borne good fruit. They have adults in their lives whom they speak to about things they may not bring to us. They have grown up conversing with adults, so they enter in with gusto.

Largely because of my partner's work with persons who have experienced homelessness and our mutual commitment to hospitality, our children have always been around adults with mental disabilities, mental health struggles, and educations from lived experience rather than school. They have been around all kinds of political and social viewpoints and a diversity of nationalities, ethnicities, and races. It is beautiful to see them defer to, interact with, and value people from all walks of life. They slip through different worlds—culturally, religiously, and racially—with an ease and insight my more monocultural rearing never gave me, however I may aspire to it.

For many of us, diversity must be sought out, and it may demand the social relocation of our families. This is neither easy nor comfortable. Building open communities in a time when people have so many ways to select and create homogeneous communities—virtual or real—takes intention, but the fruit is rich.

It was very important to us to give our children a connection to sacred Scripture. We read the Bible, discussed its oft-puzzling stories, and gave them the poetic, just visions of the prophets and the compassion and openness of Jesus. We tried to show them that our relationship to Scripture is one in which we can tussle and interrogate.

Breaking the Good-Bad Paradigm

Will and I only slowed our work of public witness so much when we became parents. We are not by any means tireless activists, but we do try to vote with our presence. Our kids, from a very young age, were taken to demonstrations for racial justice and gun control and rallies against war and others. These were always occasions to explain to them in age-appropriate language what we were working for so that our toddlers, and then children, might understand. We wanted them to realize that our search for justice needs our bodies and that it is very important to visibly stand for that which you believe in.

We stressed that some people felt differently from us and were not bad people. We said that resistance is a freedom in our country and that many people have fought for that freedom.

I carefully avoided the easy good guy–bad guy paradigm, although it is often core to children (and adult) narratives. It is important for children to realize from an early age that people are not good or bad but a complicated mix.

I believe even young children can grasp this, because at young ages, they feel both bad and good. They know that sometimes they feel happy and good in their skin, and other times they lash out and feel mean. Whether your child has just hit another, or taken someone's coveted toy without asking, or disobeyed a direct ask from you, this becomes a way to talk about how we all do bad things for different reasons and to discuss ways relationship can be restored.

Core to my own spiritual life, especially to my activism, is a truth I first grasped in Dr. Martin Luther King's principles of nonviolence, in which King taught that friendship and the capacity to *understand* the enemy was fundamental to the creation of beloved community. My enemy might carry a piece of truth I cannot see and without which I cannot be whole. This is the cornerstone I use to break my rocks of certainty and judgment. The prophet-activist in me can drench my opponents in evil, but Dr. King's admonition forces me instead on that far more difficult path—to look for that truth that they carry and that I do not see. That said, the complexity of analysis or belief we offer our children should be age appropriate. (Although age-appropriate dialogue was not my strong suit.) I do believe that children need to grow into their own questions. They do not need to be given ours. As parents, some of us may know intimately—or have grown up in—faith-steeped worlds in which we were not allowed to interrogate the Scripture, where God always had the right plan that we could not question, where theology was black and white, and a kind of orthodoxy of belief prevailed. Many of us spent a long time recovering from such worlds, and we do not want that belief system for our children. But sometimes our wavering answers mean that our children lack the sure framework they need.

At young ages, children need a God who feels certain rather than complex. God needs to be reliable and trustworthy. Children need to feel that love supports them, that the universe will hold them, and that God is powerfully with them. Imaginary friends are instinctive to children and are powerful relationships of belonging, so God makes sense as an ally. We do not necessarily need to communicate to them our spiritual questions, false certainties, and blurred edges—they will find their own, and ours may never apply. After all, they are growing up in an age different from the one we did.

This is a lesson that was delivered to me by an insightful church friend. I was on a feminist rant about inclusive language, specifically the patriarchal language of the King James translation of the Bible (the unquestioned preference of my predominantly Black church). She countered, "As a Black woman whose people have been oppressed for generations, I *need* a God who is powerful. I *need* my God to be a King, a Ruler, to embody whatever attributes of power our system gives. And if that is male, I need male. I understand where you are coming from, but my needs are different from yours." It was an eye-opening moment. I was foisting on her a judgment about how "woke" she was, but it was actually a stumbling block to the journey of empowerment she was on.

Spiritual Tools

The best things we can offer to our children are the spiritual tools that have been meaningful to us. I believe that our intention here is more important than any "right way" of doing so. Parents should think about what has been valuable to them and how they can imagine offering those things to their children.

In our case, we gave them our faith tradition, centered on the love and healing modeled by Jesus, the ancient stories and prayers, and time to discuss them. We gave them community—we had a life with lots of people in it, and we towed them along in that gift and chaos. We aspired to listen to them well—and sometimes we actually did. We tried to offer them lenses on the perspectives and needs of others, because children are naturally self-oriented as a hardwired survival skill. (And so are we.) We tried to feed their own creativity, which is a stream of God in them.

As my children got older, it was very important to me to respond to their searching questions rather than correct them with adult information. I believed it was important to be truthful about difficult things in the world while sharing at a level they could understand. While I did not want my children to grow up thinking the world was a shadowy and untrustworthy place or knowing fully the atrocities human beings are capable of devising, it was inevitable that they would encounter death, loss, and violence. When they did, I did not hide it from them with euphemism or sugarcoating. We talked in simple terms about difficult situations, answering only the questions they were content to ask.

Holy Time

What, then, to give them? I found that children, who above all love celebration and imagination, can be very nurtured by the observance of the spiritual rhythms of the year. If your tradition has these rhythms, try to use them creatively and meaningfully. I borrowed heavily from *To Dance with God* by Gertrud Mueller Nelson, the hands-down best resource I know for making the Christian liturgical year meaningful for kids. It includes lots of ideas that make the seasons both concrete and special. Advent,

Christmas, Epiphany, Lent, Easter, Pentecost, Ordinary Time, and later All Saints' Day or Day of the Dead—the cycle has deep spiritual meaning that our culture of commercialism has largely tried to hijack. In order to "clean up" for consumer culture, all the spiritual aspects of these traditions necessarily had to be stripped out, abandoned, and forgotten. Evangelical Christianity also abandoned these ancient rhythms.

From an early age, my children grasped holy time. They loved gathering around candlelight, reading a simple Scripture, singing a song they knew. The church seasons folded into the seasons of the earth, which made sense to them. This also gave me ways to redeem celebrations that our culture had coopted and infused with materialism. We were particularly vigilant around Christmas traditions—such a difficult celebration to wrest from the culture! And if you really want a puzzle, try to bring together the Easter bunny and a story of execution and resurrection.

More important than these big festivals, though, is the rhythm of the day and evening. We did the simple frames I was offered by my own family: Prayer at meals—never rote, always springing from the particular day. A snatch of a psalm in the morning and a blessing as our children went out the door, given to me by a friend: "Bless your mind for learning and creativity, your eyes for seeing beauty, your lips for speaking truth, your heart for loving and being loved, and your hands for creating beauty and justice in this world." In the evening, sharing about the day at supper, closing the day with a reading. Never preaching. Short-sentence prayers got them more comfortable with prayer.

We also read literature as a family in the evenings, especially as the kids grew older. It was a generous fifteen to thirty minutes during which we made our way through books they might not read alone but that they followed with enthusiasm when read to. Today, my kids still credit the endless books they were exposed to as a significant factor in shaping their understanding of many kinds of people. It was not having the "right" list of books, or politically correct books, that shaped their faith and their commitments to justice. Instead, it was being surrounded by so many kinds of books, cultures, characters—a fabric of rich books—that helped them appreciate the movement and diversity.

The Skill to Navigate

As parents, we have many pressures upon us—economic stresses; a plethora of too many choices around, well, everything; the struggle to find time; and the commitments we have for justice and good work. This makes it easy to cede the work of educating our children, spiritually and mentally, to other institutions.

If there were only one lesson I would spout, just one quality of good-enough parenting, it would be this: we need to spend—no, *squander* time with our kids, really listening and conversing with them, *being* with them more than *doing* with them. For those of us with privilege, this may require cultural resistance to time scarcity and work overload. It may mean we live on less than the culture tells us is necessary. Living in the world as if time were flexible and abundant is one of the greatest gifts you can offer your children.

This is more important than always having children around the "right" perspectives. Sometimes progressives—especially white, privileged progressives—want the brew to be perfect. They don't want to be in a Black church that might be more theologically conservative or a values-based, relational school that reflects fundamentalist messages. They want all the liberation messages to line up—progressive on the environment, race, gender understandings, economic liberation, vegan diets, and more.

We lefty progressives have done our critical analysis and arrived at our answers, and they are correct, by God! (And clearly, they are the only recipe to save the world.) If I devolve into political name-calling, this is precisely the rigidity "conservatives" critique in "liberals" in this country. I think the critique is well-founded. The left can carry a deep intolerance and exude the annoying certainty that we know more than other people, and our consciously raised children mirror this.

Instead of pursuing these purist brews of consciousness, we and our children would be better served if we bring them up living a range of human experience and cross-class and cross-racial understanding. Once you live in such spaces, certainties and judgments blur, and relationships move to the fore. This experience of the diversity of human life helps our children be truly tolerant and listen to other opinions, trying always to hear the piece of truth underneath. It promises to undermine orthodoxy, but it yields life rich with grace and wonder.

I have a wide range of (vehement) political opinions in my family. (My uncle named his dog after Trump well before he was first elected president, when there were still fifteen other conservative candidates in the race upon which he might have bestowed that honor). I also have the blessing of a lot of love in my family. This ended up being a gift, because my children grew up loving their family deeply, so later, when they had chances to hear and weigh the different political perspectives, they began to live with complexity. They knew many family members to be good people in the world. This personal relationship kept all the political demonizing and polarizing at bay. They were not always convinced, but they were open and respectful—and also learned to find their own ground.

But there is also a different choice in which we raise our children to engage the world in its immense brokenness and its soul-stopping beauty. We build them up to engage with all the questions of what it means—in this historical moment—to carry faith, to bear in our bodies the risk of something we believe is worth dying for, and to live in the way of love. That way is a path of healing—for ourselves, for one another, and for the earth.

In this model, the many conflicting messages offered by the world become terrain through which we make a path of faith. It is not about controlling all the messages our children hear. It is, rather, about giving them the skill to navigate through these different messages as they, in the ancient words of the prophet Micah, incarnate what it means to "do justice, love kindness, and walk humbly with God."

As they do this, and grow into themselves, parents face the hardest lesson of all: discovering that our children have their own path. All the intentions I brought to my parenting were only my flawed and imperfect efforts to convey values and resilience to the two children who had been entrusted to me. There is no accounting for what takes and what doesn't. There is no accounting for the specific, mysterious wiring and bent of each child.

As parents, we offered what we hoped were good things. We set a table. But in the end, our children are on their own journey, they make their own choices, and they have their own path—which almost certainly will not be one we envision for them.

This is not our path, and it will certainly not reflect our choices for them. It's a mystery, a cipher that will never be understood. Many turns may look or feel self-destructive. I once listened to a wise parent describe how she saw her daughter choose an abusive relationship with an addicted partner and plummet for three years. She explained, "I had to watch her do this, because it was her journey to make. But she reemerged from all the pain and abuse as a healer. She is truly gifted as a healer, and I know that it is precisely because of her journey that she has that power and that gift."

As parents, we always "see in a mirror only dimly," to use an image from Paul of Tarsus. We will never see the end of the road, the future that God holds at the heart for each child-adult. Our best judgments for them may be obstacles. They will not follow the paths we have set. Their times are for them to live in, and they must find their own paths of integrity, imagination, and transformation. The final release of parenting is that we must trust them to the Mercy.

Reflection Questions

1 How do I articulate the spirituality I want my children to feel?

2 How do I find spiritual tools and create sacred space for my kids when many of us were raised in churches and spiritual communities that had toxic impacts?

Part 2

Confronting the "Isms" in Our Families

Until the killing of Black men, Black mothers' sons, becomes as important to the rest of the country as the killing of a White mother's son—we who believe in freedom cannot rest until this happens.

—Ella Baker

Two-year-old Isaac sat on my lap, attentive as bodies lay on the cold sidewalk all around us. We listened to chants of "Black Lives Matter" and "Stop, I can't breathe." I started to join the chants, as I have for hundreds of protests before, but the words kept getting caught in my throat. The pain and disgust that these words even needed to be said shattered any momentary belief that things were or have ever been OK.

Across the die-in, I saw a Black mother with two kids, one around four and the other about Isaac's age. She whispered in their ears. I wondered what words she used, as I whispered words into my white child's ear. My son will never know the personal fear of systemic, racialized police violence that is built on a 450-year legacy that includes slavery, Jim Crow, and lynching. But I commit to ensuring that he will know the truth—and the work of racial justice that stands before us all.

Our lives are entwined with racism, sexism, heterosexism, ableism, and so on. Sometimes they can seep into the very fabric of our families, forcing us to look these sinister powers in the eye. And other times, it may feel possible to ignore them and keep quiet. But we must choose again and again to tell the truth and face the difficult work before us with our children.

The whispered words may be different because our work is different, depending on where we stand. But the spirit in the whispers remains the same because they move us together toward liberation.

6
Moving beyond Normativity

Family as a Haven for Authenticity, Self-Expression, and Equity

Jennifer Castro

Jennifer Castro is director of programs at the Martinez Street Women's Center in San Antonio, Texas. She has a BA in English and has enjoyed a meandering yet fulfilling career finding paid work in a variety of contexts, including community and women's health, public education, international relief and development, communications, and women's advocacy. Jenny is passionate about justice, truth, and their connection. She is a fierce mother of three remarkable children and has been married to Jake for nearly twenty years. She loves camping, authentic conversation, and a good cup of coffee.

Having and then raising children has challenged me to reflect on the religious, cultural, and social norms I was raised within. This process has helped me understand and more confidently stand in my authentic self. This shift toward authenticity has informed the way I parent my children and create space for them to be in the world.

The Sacredness of Feminine Knowing

I remember the quiet moments in the middle of my son's first night on this Earth. He looked up at me as I held him to my breast and suckled me desperately. He'd been crying for a while. "We got this," I told him. "I am your mama. You are mine, and I'm in this with you for the long haul."

We were spending the night in the little clinic in El Salvador's capital, San Salvador, where J was born. I'd labored all day and the entirety of the previous night. After well over twenty-four hours, I'd pushed my son into the world, surrounded by nurses and a doctor who didn't quite know what to do with the crazy woman kneeling on all fours on a hospital bed.

"*¡Quiero empujar!*" I'd shouted desperately. "I want to push!"

"Put your feet here," they'd encouraged, pointing to stirrups. But I knew I had to push, and it wasn't going to happen on my back. My spouse and I had been living and working in El Salvador for nearly a year, and I'd spent most of my pregnancy arguing with my ob-gyn about things like this: "I don't want to labor on my back," "I don't want to use any drugs for pain or to speed labor," "I don't want an episiotomy."

These and other requests would be difficult to discuss with any medically minded ob-gyn in English. But doing the research and translating my desires for labor and birth into Spanish— learning the Spanish words for *episiotomy* and *perineum*, *squatting* and *contractions*—was a whole other challenge for my spouse and me. We'd endured a good number of puzzled, "are you sure?" looks during our numerous prenatal visits despite bringing our research to our doctor.

After the hardest day of my life up to that point, my son and I were finally together. My spouse was asleep on the pull-out couch in our room. The on-call pediatrician was insistent that my son needed to be fed a bottle of formula. "He's obviously hungry, and you are not producing anything to give him!" he said to me in frustration.

"Give me some time," I had persisted. "I want to breastfeed." After a bit of back-and-forth, the pediatrician finally left us alone. And in those quiet moments together, without the pressure and intensity of the presence and opinions of others, my baby boy latched onto my breast and began to suck. I knew I had what he needed, and I was confident that I could give it to him.

This sense of confidence, a knowing, had been growing within me since the start of my pregnancy. As my strong, wise body did the mysterious work of creating another human from cellular dust, I began to recognize the power that is contained in the feminine body and the sacredness of feminine knowing. I began to see myself differently—recognizing and appreciating my own intuition and ways of being in the world. Gloria Anzaldúa calls this *la facultad*: "an instant 'sensing,' a quick perception arrived at without conscious knowing." My transformation had begun. I remember the clarity and the confidence that descended upon me in that moment.

I am mother.

I am woman.

I am powerful.

Something inside me had changed forever. My way of being in the world shifted. My center expanded. After a lifetime of believing that as a woman, I was less knowledgeable, less capable, less human, I began paying attention to and relying on my own wisdom and power. And although I was still a long way from knowing the myriad ways this would be true, I knew my life would never be the same.

A Reflection of God

I grew up within cultural and religious systems that communicated strict boundaries and status for women and girls. In my formative years, I'd begun to accumulate pieces of a heavy and debilitating burden that many women in conservative and fundamentalist cultures worldwide carry: shame, lack of confidence, limited aspirations, powerlessness, culpability, incompleteness, a need to be protected. The state of my soul entering young womanhood was overburdened—so much so that I couldn't even imagine a different way of being or hope for more.

Although pregnancy and birth shifted something in the way I experienced myself in the world, connecting what I knew intuitively to something I could articulate to my children has been a process. Now, fifteen years after J's birth, I am mother to not one but three remarkable human beings. J has two sisters: F was born two years after J, and M two years later. My children are stair steps, moving together through the stages of life and growth as a single unit, augmenting both the challenge and beauty of each life stage in multiples of three.

As they've grown, I've grown right along with them. What began as a shift in the way I saw myself in the world has expanded to an analysis of the systems within which we live. I understand as a Latina, a Mexican American woman, that the systems of education, of success, of justice in the United States were not made for me. I remember the moment when I realized that a number of my disappointing life experiences were more than the result of bad luck or personal failure; they were the result of systemic injustice and oppression. I felt both relief (maybe I'm not a screwup!) and hopelessness (how will I ever succeed?).

I've come to understand that systems in the United States and around the world are created for the benefit of a certain kind of people: white men. And that means the rest of us will struggle. It is inevitable. Recognizing this reality in my own life and then identifying the broader impacts of patriarchy for people worldwide—objectification and oversexualization of the female body, sexual violence, limited access to a livable wage, fewer opportunities for leadership—I am determined to empower and partner with my children to actively create a different kind of world for them.

This begins in my own home. So much of who our children will be is formed within our homes. Before they have any contact with the world through school or friends or community, our children first come to know themselves and what they value through family.

For me, deconstructing patriarchal assumptions and beliefs in my own life began with the way I saw myself. Through pregnancy and birth, I encountered the divine within my physical body. Coming from a traditional evangelical upbringing, I'd been taught that God was not feminine and women could never adequately reflect God's image. But pregnancy and birth revealed a sacred power housed within my feminine body—the power to create life.

The power of creation is something I'd only associated with God up to that point. And to recognize that divine power within myself was transformational. I began to see myself as sacred, a reflection of God, recognizing my own innate value and creating space for healing and wholeness in my life.

This is also the starting place for how I raise my kids. I work to cultivate within them a secure and whole sense of self. I want them to be true to who they are—confidently, uncompromisingly. Because it's from that place, I believe, that they can live what author Brené Brown calls "wholehearted lives": free and uninhibited, without the compulsion to oppress others or allowing themselves to be oppressed.

Authenticity

Wholeness requires internal work—wrestling with our experiences, our preconceived ideas, our pain—and we all need a safe space to do that. My spouse and I have worked to create that space for each other and for our kids. For us, authenticity is a rule. I don't put on an everything-is-okay facade when I'm working through hard stuff. As much as possible and as appropriate, I share with my kids what I'm struggling with. I'm honest about my joys and disappointments, my accomplishments and my pain.

"I'm feeling sad today."

"Can I tell you about something exciting that happened?"

"It's been a really hard week. I'm overwhelmed and tired."

These are all phrases my kids have heard before.

Several years ago, I resigned from a job unexpectedly as a result of a complicated and painful situation. I was heartbroken and felt like a failure. We talked about my disappointment in that work situation and in myself. We discussed how hard this transition would be for us as a family but that the bottom line is that we love one another and are in this together. We all look back on that time with relief that it's over and a sense of strength because we got through it together.

I want my children to recognize what wholeness is and what it's not. It doesn't mean having it all together all the time or always being happy. Wholeness means that you can see yourself as a complete person who holds wisdom, power, and strength as well as fallibility, blind spots, and weakness. You bring your whole self to the places you go and the interactions you engage in. You give yourself grace when you fail, and you care for yourself through boundaries and other self-care practices.

This is revolutionary in the world outside our home. Our culture in the United States, informed by white Anglo-Saxon Protestant ideals, especially in the professional workplace, values strength, control, steeled emotions, having the answer. In my leadership at work as well as in my home, I am committed to embodying a different reality—one that is comfortable with emotions, collaboration, and vulnerability and that is open to the knowledge and perspective that all bring to a problem.

In our house, sharing highs and lows around the dinner table has been a good way to get at the truth of our individual experiences and to share authentically with one another because it inevitably leads to questions and opportunities for deeper sharing. Creating space for deep sharing is important, especially in a society that devalues these kinds of practices for boys and men. We work to normalize vulnerability and to model authenticity and grace with ourselves and one another as we practice wholeness together.

As a mother, I am actively attentive to the ways my children move in the world, consciously reflecting back to them what I'm seeing as they practice wholeness in their lives. F often brings home stories of "school drama": which friends aren't talking to one another, who's getting on whose nerves, what so-and-so said to so-and-so. She values friendship tremendously and is a loyal friend to many people, so she struggles to make sense of the tensions that arise, feeling that so many of the arguments are simply not worth the trouble.

Once on the way home from school, she shared with me how two friends had each been complaining to her about the other. That day at lunch, as all three of them sat together, in a very sixth-grade way, F stated that she didn't want to be in the middle of their argument but that she cared very much for both girls and wanted them to work out their issues. Surprisingly, the girls were able to name their complaints to each other and decided that they too wanted a better friendship.

F told me this story, venting, to describe how very difficult and emotional her day had been. I responded with joy, "Do you realize what you did?" She looked at me incredulously. I pointed out to her how remarkable it was that she had helped her friends communicate with each other in a healthy way, bringing her skills and her love to them at a time when they needed it.

It's important for me that my kids recognize the love and power they bring to experiences and interactions by showing up whole. So I name it when I see it. I want them to be comfortable being themselves, in their own skin. I never want them to pretend to be anyone other than who they are.

Self-Expression

Self-expression is an important part of that. Often I'm trying to get the family out the door, and I'm urging, "Let's go! We're going to be late!" And one of my daughters or my son shows up in the most absolutely unexpected outfit. When they were younger, it was usually a costume (a pirate, a butterfly, a dragon), and I'd grab a change of clothes from their drawer (just in case they felt like changing while we were out). Then I'd ask, "Will you be comfortable in that? Will you be able to run?" (or play kickball, or whatever it was that we were on our way to do). Usually they said yes, even though I knew it wasn't true, and we'd load up the dragon in the car and head to our event.

These days it isn't a costume anymore. Now it's a leotard or a fancy dress, or something more appropriate for winter in one-hundred-degree heat. But my response for the most part is the same. Will you be comfortable? Self-expression is part of self-defining. How we present ourselves to the world is a key part of self-expression.

A few years ago, when my son was ten or eleven, he was really into polishing his toenails. He enjoyed the dark colors: brown, black, green. He kept it up for several months. I didn't think twice about this. It was simply how J was choosing to express his personality. But at a family get-together, some members of my extended family gave his feet some disapproving looks and even asked me, "What's up with J's toes?"

"Why would something be up?" was my response. "It's how he's expressing himself." We talked for a bit, and I did my best to explain that I am happy for my kids to express themselves how they choose through their appearance. Later, J told me a bit ashamedly that he'd been confronted by a family member about the polish. I asked how that made him feel. He named some feelings of discomfort, of disappointment, of pain. I affirmed that his body was his, and he could choose for himself how to adorn it (exceptions to this rule are, for now, piercings and tattoos, which are more permanent and so require the wisdom of age).

A few days later, J's dad polished his own toenails a bright green. And he kept it up for a few weeks. We didn't make a big deal about it, and nobody brought it up again. But J kept painting his nails for several months after that. And since then, my spouse will randomly paint his toenails every now and again. For us it's vital that our kids feel free and empowered to do what they choose with their bodies; they aren't ours to police. And we want to normalize the various ways this can happen.

A Different Way

As a family, we work to engage with one another lovingly. We understand love to be intentional, attentive, and active care for one another. It sometimes requires putting aside our own desires or priorities. When I listen to my kids talk about their favorite slime recipe (even when I'm bored out of my brains), when I drop off their homework at school when they forget it at home, when I make them a healthy dinner, when I spend time snuggling and reading with them before bed, I'm showing them love. When they indulge me in a dance party, when they do an extra chore because I'm just too tired, when they listen to me describe a tedious work meeting (even when they don't understand the details), they show me love. We practice compassion, respect, and authenticity at home so that it becomes part of who we are in the world.

Like many families, we have our good and bad days, and there is no shame in admitting when we've failed. My kids know what an authentic apology looks like; I've offered more than I can count. And the beauty comes when they begin, on their own, to offer sincere and loving apologies. "I'm sorry I said that to you, Mom. I didn't mean to hurt you." This tells me that they're beginning to recognize what love looks like and what it doesn't look like. They can distinguish between when they're being their best selves and when they're not.

Together we strive to be our best selves for one another. As we do that, our transformational work expands. It becomes about community and systemic change, about imagining and creating different systems for the benefit of not only my children but also my extended family, my community, my city, my future grandchildren, and future generations.

Systemic transformation requires that we confront the systemic realities we (both children and adults) face in our society and in the world: racism, sexism, ageism, heterosexism, ableism. By embodying love and ways of being that are in opposition to the systems we live in, we ourselves become building blocks, reimagining and then actively doing our part to create new systems.

As a family, we choose to live counterculturally. My spouse and I are doing our work (it's an ongoing process) and raising children who are critically interrogating the systems they inherited—interrupting cycles of domination that have existed within our extended families' religious and cultural systems for generations. Both my spouse and I come from families where "the man is the head of the house." Men are the breadwinners, get served by their women, and have the final say. Women are submissive and obedient.

We decided early on that we wanted something different for the family we were creating together. We wanted the culture in our house to be one of equity. Over the years, as a couple, we've shared responsibilities of earning income, paying bills, raising children, cooking and cleaning, all while making an effort to be present for each other in the busyness of getting through each day (there are definitely seasons when this is especially difficult, but it is always a goal). We do our best to model loving partnership and commitment to each other and our family. I am only healthy and thriving if *we* are healthy and thriving. If one of us is struggling, we all do what we can to support, love, and find solutions to problems together. And this collaborative way of being in our family influences the way my kids show up in the world.

From a very young age, J could accurately articulate his feelings. He's always had a strong conviction about justice and right and wrong. One year for his birthday, he asked that all his friends, instead of giving him presents, donate money to an organization that's working to save endangered species. Once after playing a ninety-minute soccer game in one-hundred-degree heat, he walked all around the bleachers picking up pieces of trash and recycling that spectators had left behind. He couldn't bear to leave them there. Through his words and actions, he is an example to his peers of a different way.

Expanding Safe Space

Sex and sexuality are common topics of conversation in our household. My spouse and I are not ashamed of our sex life around our children. Our bedroom door is rarely locked, but when it is, our kids understand and respect the fact that sometimes Mom and Dad take time to love each other in a special and private way. We teach them that sex is a natural part of a healthy relationship and, because our bodies are not shameful, we consistently call all our body parts by their appropriate names. We answer their questions honestly and with transparency and create space for healthy, open conversation about sexuality, which is happening more and more as they are transitioning from childhood into adolescence.

"Mom, what is happening with my body? Can I show you something?"

"Sure . . . Oh my, look at that [hair growing in places where it hadn't before, cervical fluid on underwear, body part getting bigger]! You're growing up! This is so exciting!" Usually, I'll explain a bit about whatever is going on with their body, and they'll ask more questions. I celebrate my kids' milestones so that they'll keep asking questions.

"Mommy, what is an STI?"

"It stands for sexually transmitted infection. That means a person can get it from another person during sexual contact or touching. It is super important that when you decide to have sex, you ask your partner about infections they might have and if they've been tested. And always, always, *always* use a condom." Yes, I say this even now. It's important that my children hear messages like this as much as possible before they begin to experience sexual passion and urges. I want my voice in their head (well, if not mine, *a* voice), reminding them of their future and well-being.

"Mom, how would two people of the same gender have sex?"

"Honestly, I'm not speaking from experience here. This has not been my reality. But I do know that there are various ways to experience sexual pleasure outside of a penis entering a vagina. The clitoris is a very sensitive part of the woman's body and can be stimulated with your hand or with your mouth. So can a man's penis. I think there are many ways to experience sexual pleasure, and that's the fun of sex: exploring this together with someone you trust."

I want my kids to understand their own bodies, to know themselves. I believe this understanding empowers them to make healthy decisions for themselves. Once as we were discussing masturbation over dinner, my spouse made a joke and my kids erupted in laughter. And through his laughter, my son said, "I'm so glad we're the kind of family who can talk about this stuff." So am I.

I'm thankful that my kids feel safe enough to talk about their crushes with me. Sometimes they crush on kids of other genders, sometimes on kids of the same gender. The first time one experienced a same-gender crush, they were clearly nervous about telling me. During a heavy silence, while I waited for them to feel comfortable, I said, "I love you. Nothing you can say will change that." Once the truth was shared, I smiled and pulled my child in for a huge hug. And then I said, "That's exciting. And it's perfectly normal to have crushes on girls and boys. You're figuring yourself out. And that's okay." When I looked at them again, I saw relief mixed with joy on their face. Since this conversation, my other kids have shared their same-gender crushes with me too—with much less trepidation and a lot more confidence.

I'm so glad my children can count on one safe space where they can express their feelings and be who they are. But I also recognize that they live in the world—in Texas, in our case. Our extended family is still our family, and my kids encounter plenty of messages that communicate a lot of unhealthy things about people who are LGBTQ. My spouse and I do our best to counter those messages in the things we do and say, as well as the people we choose to surround ourselves with. My hope is that as we love and accept our children for who they are and where they are, creating safe spaces for them, they will feel strengthened and empowered to create those kinds of safe spaces for others in the world outside our home.

My kids aren't dating yet, but my hope is that we have created a safe landing place for them to process future relationship joys and struggles and that they will continue to ask questions. And when they're ready for sex with another person, I hope we can process that step with them too. I want to give them the confidence to name their needs and boundaries. I want sex for them to be not about pressure or "cool points" but about pleasure and sharing and joy.

When I first became a mother, a wise person told me that when we look at the big picture, our primary job as parents is letting our kids go, little by little, over the course of a couple of decades. At first this idea terrified me, because I love my kids more than I've loved anyone and anything in my life. As a mother, I want them to be safe. I want them to be happy. I want them to be whole.

But I also realize that these precious and fleeting years are such an opportunity. I can create for my kids a safe and loving space to understand themselves and the world, to figure out what they value and who they are. As they gain confidence in those things, I can let them go, little by little. And then I can stand back and watch them be—in awe of who they've become, thankful for their wisdom, perspective, and partnership in creating a different world together.

I'm thankful that I get to walk with my kids in life. I'm thankful for these formative years. And I'm thankful for the honor of being their mother.

Reflection Questions

1 What transformations have happened in me that put me in a more powerful position to parent for my kids, embracing all of who they are?

2 How does my family provide space to push boundaries around gender?

3 How do I create a safe, loving environment for my kids to express themselves?

7
Raising Antiracist White Kids

Some Rules Need to Be Broken

Jennifer Harvey

Jennifer Harvey is a writer, educator, and public speaker. Her work focuses on encounters between religion and ethics, race, gender, activism, politics, spirituality, and just about every other area of social life in the United States. Her greatest passion continually returns her to racial justice and white antiracism work. She engages with faith communities, nonprofits, and other groups seeking to deepen their justice commitments. She teaches full time in Drake University's Philosophy and Religion Department and is the author of *Raising White Kids: Bringing Up Children in a Racially Unjust America* (Abingdon, 2018).

I have to acknowledge that what I most want to be as a parent is good. There is in this understandable longing, however, much to be untangled and unlearned if we are to engage the urgent work of antiracist-committed parenting. For white parents, this includes learning to break white silence, which is a difficult challenge because white silence has been part of our own socialization, a racial habit handed down through generations. It also includes recognizing the many places where white supremacy pervades white cultures' notions of good, right, or even true in ways that can actually undermine antiracist development and values in our kids. When we begin to recognize its presence in some of these places, we can start to change and transform the ways we engage in them with our children, enabling them to grow a moral capacity for antiracism.

P arenting is hard. It's beautiful. It brings unexpected joys. Almost every day, parenting is interesting. It's always sacred. But if there's a laugh I can count on when I talk to communities about the work of raising antiracist white children, it comes when I tell folks, "I was a much, much better parent . . . before I actually became one." Because parenting is really, really hard.

The reasons parenting is hard start with how physically grueling it is when our kiddos are tiny (you couldn't pay me now to knowingly go back to that kind of sleep deprivation). They continue with the unfolding recognition that there's so much we don't know and always more we need to learn in order to parent well. Meanwhile, we're not always sure what "well" means or whether what we're doing will help things turn out that way.

To top it off, there's the emotional and spiritual work of living with the reality that even when we do our best, parent-child relationships are impacted by so many factors, many of which we can't control. Our kids have their own personalities. Our young people have their own experiences. And every day, the communities and worlds we live in blast them with all kinds of values and claims.

At the center of many of the dynamics that make the wonderful experience of parenting challenging for me sits a deep longing. What I most want to be as a parent is *good*. Yet I'm wrestling with the realization that there's so much to be untangled and unlearned as we engage this urgent work of antiracist-committed parenting. One kind of work has to do with questioning assumptions about some of our most fundamental values and moral lessons—things that seem as basic as the longing to be good.

A Few Principles First

Several principles and priorities are immediately relevant when it comes to raising white children and youth who are committed to racial justice. An overarching principle is that white parents have to learn to break white silence; we need to commit hard to doing so, over and over again. White silence has long pervaded the ways white families have nurtured our young. It's been handed down generationally and persists today. Versions of this silence include everything from so-called color blindness, to vague abstractions like "everyone's equal," to saccharine teachings about celebrating differences. Its long-term impact has rendered even those of us who long to be committed to justice very far behind, as generational silence has impeded our own antiracist capacities as well our collective ability to engage and mentor white youth for antiracism.

Countless studies have measured the degree to which white families fail to explicitly teach about race and racism, in stark contrast to families of color. They have also clearly documented the impact of this failure. Children internalize racism from their earliest developmental moments. In this way, white silence is the equivalent of, as Beverly Daniel Tatum says, failing to give our kids breathing masks before sending them out into the world each day to inhale polluted, smog-filled air.

Parenting for antiracism requires white parents to break silence by talking early and often about race, racism, and antiracism. When it comes to racism, we need to go beyond talking about it and specifically teach our children to recognize it. We need to help them grow their moral muscles by envisioning with them how they can respond when they encounter it. When it comes to antiracism, not only do we need to talk and teach about it. *We need to model antiracist behaviors in our day-to-day lives.*

In the long arc of wrestling to break white silence in my own life and in my parenting, I continue to discover places where white silence shows up in ways that are insidious. This brings me back to the need to reconsider some of the most basic parenting messages through the lens of antiracist impact.

There Is No Generic Anything

Teaching basic values—such as kindness, compassion, and goodness—seems like Parenting 101. And in some ways it is.

Nothing I say here should be construed as advocating that we teach our kids values that are the opposite of being good or kind, or that starting with goodness and kindness isn't important. But I want to illustrate ways that seemingly generic approaches to values are not enough.

Antiracism and racial justice can't grow from soil with even the deepest tilling of generic moral values. Values posited in general forms—or taught in a universal, one-size-fits-all way—can only be stepping-stones at best. They are not the complete journey. They are meaningful only to the extent that we use them as steps to persistently move toward increasingly specific and nuanced teachings.

Because we are living lives in which structural injustices create radically different experiences if we are white—in contrast to those we have if we are Black, Native, Latinx, Asian, or multiracial—generic values *just aren't a thing*. Universal truths don't exist either. Values only meaningfully exist in the very *particular forms* they take as we pursue them in complicated and inequitable social, educational, geographical, and political contexts.

I want to go one step further. In contexts where white supremacy pervades and impacts the character of white cultures (which in turn socializes those of us who are white), notions of *good*, *right*, or even *true* (again, all Parenting 101 values) can actually undermine antiracist development and values in our kids. Unlearning such notions—better put, complicating them—is thus profoundly important. I want to illustrate what I'm getting at by reflecting on three common teachings lots of us parents (like me!) use.

Treat Others the Way You Want to Be Treated (Kindness)

The Golden Rule would seem an unassailably solid way to teach children to be kind. "Do unto others as you would have them do unto you" presents itself as a universal and universalizable test kids can rely on to assess their own behavior.

But let's consider the problems it can create through an example. I am a hugger. For me, expressions of greeting, friendship, mutual regard, or appreciation for a positive collective experience are captured no better than by sharing a hug. But it's not difficult to realize the implications of turning my experience into a universal measure for behavior. The Golden Rule implies I can assume that because hugs feel great to me, I should hug other people no matter what—and they should like it.

Obviously, this would be a dangerous application. And I've learned, of course, that not everyone wants to participate in hugging. Fortunately, parents are increasingly learning to teach kids basic respect for the profound differences among us when it comes to the boundaries and experiences of our bodies—not to mention building the scaffolding kids need in order to understand consent (their own and others'). No one person's experience of hugging should be projected onto another. So like many parents, I'm teaching my kids that they need to inquire into and then honor what the experience of a hug would mean to the other person.

The Golden Rule's good intent is to activate a sense of empathy. It's intended to encourage children to pause and notice what it would be like to be on the receiving end of a particular form of treatment. But this is also precisely the problem with it. As my hugging example shows, it's inadequate and even risky to teach kids to use their own experiences as a proxy for the experience of others.

A much better formulation of the Golden Rule begins with radical particularity. "Do unto others as *they would have you* do unto them." We can only understand what others would have us do by inquiring into their needs, desires, and experiences and then honoring those as best we can.

This difference is not semantics. How we teach white kids values couldn't be more important. Whiteness, and the insulations and unjust access that wrap around the daily experience of living while white, make it risky to strip values of their universality and root them in particularity.

Writer Ijeoma Oluo helps us understand why. Oluo digs into what's going on when white people minimize reports of racism they hear from people of color. "Are you sure that was about race?" is an endlessly common response to reports of such incidents. One of the things going on, says Oluo, is that white people project their own experiences of the world onto people of color. We think, "How could that be about race? If it happened to me, it wouldn't have been!" Never mind that most of us have literally no idea, or merely abstract intellectualized ones, about what people of color actually live every single day.

None of this means that we have to throw out the value of kindness, and this isn't overly complicated. Kids can be taught to stop and inquire before drawing conclusions about what something is like for another person. They can be taught that kindness is most kind when it comes in a form in which another person experiences it as such. Meanwhile, this teaching brings the added benefits of necessitating that our kids learn the basic habit of inquiry and curiosity, along with the skills to demonstrate these respectfully. It works against the temptation to presume we know what others need without having to find out.

The power and privileges afforded to white people mean that from the youngest of ages, being listened to, taken seriously, heard, and responded to are part of white formation. This experience varies with other identity factors—such as gender, gender identity, sexual orientation, and physical ability—but the whiteness piece pertains even for those of us who live identities in which other kinds of marginalization are part of our formation. Regardless of whether we understand the "why" behind someone else's experience, by starting with the particulars of their experience—instead of assumptions about universal experiences—we can learn to decenter ourselves when deciding what behaviors are good or desirable. And the practice of decentering the white experience over and over again and learning to ask about, listen to, and learn from the experiences of others could not be more urgent.

Listen to Your Teacher (Respect)

We use another seemingly foolproof universal to teach the value of respect: "Listen to your teacher!" Of course, respect matters. We need to support our kids in growing habits that make them good members of a community—which is what a classroom is. How our kids show up at school impacts the ways a learning environment can be nurtured in spaces where there are lots of bodies (and energy!) in one room.

But a longer view is important here for at least two reasons. First, few children attend schools where antiracist lenses are thorough and actively deployed in teaching and learning. Second, conformity and compliance get transmitted and taught through messages about listening to authorities.

I've shared in other places about the time my daughter was learning about George Washington at school. I wrestled to find an entrée point to complicate this teaching without shaming my second grader or shutting down her enthusiasm about learning. Then one morning she overheard a conversation on the radio about adults who "do bad things"—hard for her to believe—and the door opened. I pointed her back to George Washington as an example. I told her that he had enslaved African people. After being horrified to learn this, my daughter turned to the more relevant concern in her life: "Why did my teacher talk about him like he was so great?"

Whitewashed versions of US history get transmitted in schools daily. This is not just a problem of incomplete facts. It's a problem of ingesting smog that harms your body. George Washington taught only as a hero to an eight-year-old malforms the developing white mind in ways that create serious challenges as that mind continues to develop. And this, of course, is just one example.

Our children need to learn to question their teachers. They need to question them directly, not only because this is a way to invite classrooms to have more truth-filled and nuanced teachings about race and racism, but because it's also critical for building the moral muscle to question authority, which takes strength. Conformity and compliance, and unquestioning respect for authority, are the opposite of what antiracism requires in this racially unjust society.

When I first publicly wrote about this discussion with my daughter in an op-ed piece for the *New York Times*, the most frequent defensive white response I received was the accusation that I was judging George Washington by the standards of our day—because in his day, the logic went, he was just doing what was accepted. This is itself a whitewashed way of reading the past. People of African descent knew enslavement was wrong. So did lots and lots of white US Americans. A few fought it, many tolerated it, and many others enslaved people despite knowing it was wrong.

But beyond that, something deeper strikes me here. Those defensive messages valorize the idea that it is perfectly acceptable that Washington would conform to the expectations of his time. Believing that we shouldn't even name, let alone morally judge, the past creates a present-day teaching that Washington's conformity (if not his enslaving ways) was a case of doing the right thing.

A powerful and dangerous alignment exists here between that specious argument about the past and the kind of conformity we are actively teaching our kids today when we repeat "listen to your teacher" without the supportive, nuanced specificity and modeling of why questioning authority is important. Breaking with practices and "the way things are" today is exactly what white people (all of us) need to do! Not only does giving folks like Washington a pass distort historical truths; it also teaches our kids that conformity is laudable in an unjust world.

There's more discussion to be had about how we teach our kids to question authority in ways that are respectful, in classrooms and elsewhere. On this front, we may need to grow our adult moral imaginations. But the reality remains: kids need to learn to question authority, and school is one of the primary places conformity is taught—including, but not only, through the dissemination of pervasively whitewashed school curriculums.

Parenting for antiracism thus requires thinking through how white kids can learn to respect their beloved teachers without respecting racist myths and practices. Such moral creativity might actually be a gift to teachers, who are themselves embedded in systems that put them in the difficult position of teaching racist myths. Dissent and questioning are healthy and good for all of us. They are nonnegotiable if we want a different world.

Always Follow the Rules (Obedience)

It's long been present, but since 2016, the language of "law and order" has been louder and shriller. It's been invoked to commit the most heinous acts of racial violence and human rights violations. And so many parents are struggling to figure out how to speak about these things, because we know our kids are breathing them in.

In this context, one of the most pervasive early developmental teachings—"follow the rules"—stands out as one that needs to be particularized and made nuanced early. For, when deployed in the context of unjust racial systems, the moral formation that this so-called generic, universally applicable message presents becomes a weapon of white supremacy.

Some of the most egregious violations of life in communities of color were and are "legal." Antiracism necessitates challenging, organizing against, and sometimes even breaking laws. "Following the rules" is the kid version of believing the law is always right and has the final word. We have to address this when kids are very young.

One way white parents can begin to do this is to consider how we talk about racial justice leaders with our kids and youth. We valorize people like Rosa Parks and Rev. Dr. Martin Luther King Jr. both at home and at school, and we teach our kids to do the same. Honoring them is of course appropriate, but valorizing them without engaging the larger context in which they acted does a disservice to their actual legacies and whitewashes the civil rights movement more broadly. It also misses a compelling opportunity to teach our children the lesson that morality is more important than the law.

We might easily ask young children to wonder aloud with us about why that white bus driver in Montgomery decided that following the rules was more important than respecting people's basic dignity and rights. We might also ask them to think about the moral courage and commitment it took for Parks to break the law. Do our kids know that Dr. King not only went to jail but also encouraged other people to break the law and go to jail? Regular, sustained conversations on such topics are critically important for complicating the strong messages kids get about following the rules and obeying the law. Not only do such explorations give them room to flex their moral muscles and think about their own willingness to do racially just or unjust things; they also help them start to recognize that laws can be unjust and evil.

White culture in the United States has long conflated what is legal with what is moral. This has always been dangerous. It has become pointedly so for children and youth growing up in contexts now where law is running amok over basic principles of decency and humanity. It couldn't be more important that we find explicit ways to teach our children the difference between what is lawful and what is right.

Our morality must be rooted in loyalties to justice, humanity, and truth that run deeper than our loyalty to law. While that may be easy for us to remember as adults, it's every bit as important that we pass the same message on to our children.

Let's Return to the Good

I close with two brief reflections about us adults. Raising white kids in a way that, collectively, they and we have not been raised before is a massive responsibility. It's also an unknown journey, because white people haven't generationally done this work before. We long so deeply to be *good* at this.

But an obsession with being good can itself become a weapon of whiteness. It's long been recognized by people of color that white people's desire to be perceived by them as "good," or as an exception, harms personal and political/coalitional interracial relationships. We must long to do what is good (in this case— justice) more strongly than we obsess about looking good.

When it comes to my parental longing, this is true in a related but deeper way. The desire to be good can so easily get in the way of taking the risk, having the conversation, pushing the envelope into developing new and different parental habits in order to raise antiracist white kids. My longing to be good is partly rooted in wanting my kids to thrive in the world, yes. But it's also sometimes about wanting to not make mistakes, to have easy answers, and to adhere to sets of easy-to-follow practices. This desire to be good gets in the way, because doing something new and difficult will always bring mistakes, and action must come even before we know exactly how to do all of this right.

Antiracist parenting requires courage and bravery. It means loosening my grip on my desire to be good.

So I close with a word of love, as I acknowledge that this sacred work of parenting for antiracism is hard: Find yourself some people who are in it with you. Find other adults contending with these difficult questions, attempting to root out and be clear about where the subtle, insidious outcomes of whiteness manifest in the most taken-for-granted of parental habits. Find yourself a community of people who you can have on speed dial when you need them to help you become ever more deeply attuned and who will help you brainstorm and be accountable—but who also will love and support you as you practice bravery and courage.

If you can find people who physically live near you, who can also be adults your kids have access to—all the better. Our kids need other adults of many different racial groups from whom to receive nuanced, particular, open-ended inquiries and teachings. This will embolden them to live against the grain of the normative white, racist compliance and presumptions that are formative in all white lives.

Find yourself some people. Because parenting is hard. It is unexpectedly joyful. It is never dull. It is sacred and beautiful. But it is hard. And we all need one another to ground, support, and nurture us in this most transformative work.

Reflection Questions

1 What do I find most challenging about imagining teaching kids in my life to question authority and even rules and laws?

2 Are there other generic, universal messages I unwittingly pass on and need to rethink in a commitment to the antiracist socialization of white children and youth?

8

Resisting Patriarchy

Messy, Beautiful Interdependence

Sarah and Nathan Holst

Sarah and Nathan Holst live in the Tischer Creek Watershed in Duluth, Minnesota. They center queer, racial, and environmental justice in their work of movement building and creating relational, healing spaces. Out of connection to place and commitment to truth-telling within legacies of trauma and resilience, Nathan "catches" songs and Sarah writes and creates visual art. In their journey of being new parents to baby Sage, they incorporate what they have learned about being fully human in a hurting world while together visioning and embodying restoration.

Navigating patriarchy in cross-gender partnerships can be challenging—and all the more challenging when you layer in parenting children, especially knowing that parents teach primarily through modeling. In this piece, we explore themes and questions that arise as we engage deeply with parenting and patriarchy: What is the difference between patriarchy and the person embodying it? How do we make it so that we can both bring in what we are fully experiencing and support one another as full, feeling human beings, even as we know patriarchy is playing into the dynamics at hand? How do we distinguish what is a personal difference in values or style and what is unjust gendered conditioning? What follows is our exploration of these questions and themes through reflection and a shared conversation. Though we write this first section together, there are times when we use our names in the third person to designate particular aspects of our experience and to center both sets of experiences, practicing the equity we hope is embodied in this piece.

The Challenge

The process of navigating patriarchy during the first year of our child Sage's life has been significant. Subscribing to the idea that our personal lives are the first arena where we can transform our political realities, we have been trying to usher in a new world through the intentional act of parenting equitably. After a year of check-ins around the differences in our roles and the balance of engagement in organizing and parenting labor, we have few answers, but we do have examples of experiments we have tried and questions we are asking.

We are white people in our thirties living in Duluth, Minnesota. We both inhabit queer identities, though our relationship is straight-passing. Nathan is the main monetary provider for our family through his work as a faith formation minister at a United Church of Christ. Sarah is a master's student and artist and contributes money here and there. We are in an income bracket in which we qualify for government assistance, but we are rich in social capital, with both sets of our parents living in our neighborhood and with access to extended community support.

Like the author bell hooks, we understand patriarchy as "institutionalized sexism." In order to stop it, we need individuals and communities to "let go of sexist thoughts and actions." This is no small task. It is radical and transformational work, because these systemic beliefs and behaviors are entrenched.

Like many in our generation and beyond, we believe that if we learn to recognize and call out sexism when we see it, not only will it be a step toward toppling the larger structure of patriarchy, but it also will help free us to become fully loving humans who know ourselves and our communities deeply. This is what patriarchy tries to take away from all of us. Patriarchy, like all kinds of intersecting oppressions, gets in the way of loving relationships.

Simply put, we desire and need loving relationships that allow all of us to be our most powerful and beautiful selves. We want that for ourselves, and we want it for our children. We want it for our communities and for the readers of this book. We believe the work of dismantling patriarchy will move us there because we have already begun to experience these results in our family.

We make time for a weekly relationship check-in (often while we are on a walk with Sage in the stroller), during which we reflect on our division of labor and emotional well-being and determine if anything needs to shift. Because patriarchy follows patterns in which men expect emotional support from women, we check in with each other before launching into processing, which requires the other person's emotional labor. We listen intentionally to each other.

We name and affirm how raising a child is of equal or greater importance (and difficulty) as working a job outside the home is. We share the labor of cleaning and tidying, even if Nathan might not prioritize clean space in the same way that Sarah does. We are moving toward a practice of sharing the labor of meal-planning. We periodically engage in another counterpatriarchal practice: going to couples therapy. Through this, Nathan often relearns that he "can't fix it," and Sarah gets a need filled by hearing how much Nathan loves and appreciates her.

It is often easier for folks socialized male to prioritize their self-care than it is for folks socialized as female, so we are getting better at centering Sarah's self-care as we plan our weeks. Instead of waiting for Sarah to delegate child-related tasks, Nathan has started to learn how to recognize when something needs to be done and to offer to do it.

Looking back, we see that the seeds of our current questions have been around since the beginning of our parenting journey. We were as intentional as possible. During labor, Nathan sang birth songs and swayed with Sarah through waves of contractions. After the birth, we were surrounded by the support of Sage's grandparents and community. We even made the decision that Nathan would stay up at night alongside Sarah as Sage nursed. Nathan read books aloud to ground us in our new call: *Braiding Sweetgrass* and *Revolutionary Mothering*.

When the grandparents left and we were on our own, a sleep-deprived Nathan labored with feeling uncharacteristically angry and powerless. This all culminated at two o'clock one morning as we were passing a bright red and screaming Sage back and forth. Nathan, delirious from exhaustion, emoted his anger in a way that Sarah experienced as directed at Sage. After Sage was finally back to sleep, Sarah stewarded the conflict: "I know the timing is terrible, but we have to talk about what is going on."

The subsequent exploration brought out themes we were familiar with from facilitating racial and environmental justice work together: How do we make it so that we can both bring in what we are fully experiencing and support one another as full, feeling human beings, even as we know patriarchy is playing into the dynamics at hand? How do we distinguish what is a personal difference in values or style and what is unjust gendered conditioning?

Conversations and honest check-ins have been a strength in our relationship. We offer this transcribed conversation, recorded on a car trip in the middle of our writing process for this chapter, as a model for ways to have complicated, vulnerable, loving conversations. We have learned the most from the people in our lives who have been willing to share their experiences deeply and vulnerably, and we hope that this conversation might illuminate insights and ideas on how you can explore resisting patriarchy in your own parenting relationships.

The Conversation

SARAH: One thing that has been coming up for me as we do this project is wanting to stay grounded in our own struggles and questions rather than assuming that we are really good at this. I have some anger and resentment toward you rising to the surface when I think about the first few weeks of Sage's life.

During those first weeks, you would frequently take breaks to trim the cedar trees in our backyard. This was our first parenting experience in balancing the dynamic of how you often need to have your own separate time apart in order to feel restored and be present. However, being the person whose body made a baby and who was breastfeeding, I did not have that same early opportunity to have alone time. I find myself looking back and asking the question, Was that unfair? Would we shift that in the future? What does equitable parenting mean when our roles are very different?

NATHAN: In hearing you share, the question I bring is, What is my role in listening to this? Do I just say, "Hey, I hear you, I am listening, and that makes sense"? Do you need a listening ear or an apology?

SARAH: I want you to reflect on that time and how you might be thinking about it differently, now that I have shared my experience and with a whole year of parenting under your belt. Would you still relate to that time in a similar way, say, if we had a second child?

NATHAN: I guess I'll say first that sometimes it's just about noticing just how entrenched patriarchy is. In some ways, I've gotten used to the responses in my body during conversations. There is immediate resistance in me: "I don't want to do that! I just did my thing, and isn't that enough?" I need to first take a deep breath and prepare myself to go back to that time and do a little internal work. I definitely feel my emotional walls going up, and I have to actively try to take them down.

It's been a little over a year, and that initial period of Sage's life is very blurry for me. I remember feeling that it was just incredibly hard—much harder than I thought it would be. I had not experienced that kind of sleep deprivation in the past, and I felt like every moment was a huge challenge. I remember thinking, "God, I just need to get outside and have a few moments to trim the cedar trees." Your parents were around, so it felt like that was possible.

But it's still true that it is inherently unequal when you're the one that nurses. There are some really incredible experiences of connection within that, which I don't experience, but I also have a little more freedom during those times when I can't really do much to help. Does that mean I should, or get to, go out and do a restorative practice so that I can come back refreshed?

Sometimes it is difficult to suss out. If we imagined a world where patriarchy didn't exist, would this conversation be similar? Would you be willing to let me take a break, or would you still feel that it was unfair and that you wanted me to stay with you, even though I might do better if I went out?

SARAH: Hearing you remember that time as being really blurry is hard. I have a sense of real sweetness and joy when I think about that time, in addition to it being hard. There's a piece of me that is asking why we don't share that memory of joy. I want to share that sweetness with you and not have that time be remembered only as a really hard time. I felt surprised, given our relationship to gender norms and our queerness, that there was such a binary, where I was the more nurturing one. I felt like I rose to parenting in a different way from the way you did.

NATHAN: I think that's true. What strikes me is that I thought I would rise to it as well.

SARAH: I think we both expected that.

NATHAN: What I discovered was sleep-deprived Nathan. Looking back on it, I think I was kind of angry that I wasn't enjoying it more. Maybe what drew me to the restorative practice was that it helped me get a little closer to enjoying that time. What I found was that I can be more present when I have time by myself as well. Of course, there were times when I did enjoy us being together, but the times when I didn't somehow feel stronger. I wish they didn't.

SARAH: That's so hard to know what to do with. And it does feel like a larger parent pattern of people socialized as male not being there. I think about our friends Elaine and John. John built all those garden beds and a back fence while he was on paternity leave, because he saw time off as a time to do projects. That time should be about learning parenting roles together.

But I also don't want to fault you. Had I experienced postpartum depression, we would have made space for me. I think what you experienced was something very similar to that: something like adjustment-to-parenting depression. I want to give you space to absolutely deal with your mental health in a new season of life in appropriate ways. And I also felt abandoned in that season that I was really hoping that we could share together.

NATHAN: The reason I want to end patriarchy is that I want to know: Is what I experienced based on my socialization and what patriarchy has instilled in me, or is that just a part of who I am? Maybe it's not that important to know the answer, because my experience and the impact it had on you still happened. If we are thinking about next time, do I just work through it and not take time away? Do we make a plan for me to have regular time on my own? Will that avoid falling into patterns of gendered patriarchal roles?

Do you have thoughts on that?

SARAH: One thing that will be different is that we'll have a different expectation going in next time. We'll know that potentially it will be hard for you. I don't know if you'll react similarly the second time, but if you do, I think we'll have a different set of tools. We do have community that we can rely on. I can feel closeness and sharing with grandparents and people that aren't experiencing the same kind of sleep deprivation and anger. Finding ways to get my needs met without expecting that from you feels like a way that we could handle it.

I feel like we both need to push to dismantle what we can and also make sure we're both really cared for. The other piece is that I don't necessarily feel like I wasn't cared for. It would be very different saying "I wasn't cared for" than saying "I wish you had enjoyed it with me."

NATHAN: Because I did show up, right?

SARAH: You did. You really did. You stayed up and read books, which was a sweet piece of that time. You got up with me every single time that Sage got up. You were actively engaged, but you weren't enjoying it. That's a hard thing to know what to do with.

NATHAN: Right! Do I just fake it until I make it? I don't think so. Sometimes I can shift my thinking, but I don't want to say I love it when I'm actually in despair.

The other piece that I was thinking about was your feeling of being abandoned. That seems connected to gendered patriarchal experiences. How do we get at that? I think about the question, What can you count on me for? I can let you know what I'm planning and be clear about how you can count on me. Is that a helpful framing?

SARAH: I don't know. There's a power imbalance in that framing. I don't want to have to ask you for support. I wish the whole thing was shared.

NATHAN: Much more mutual.

SARAH: Yes.

NATHAN: And enjoyment is part of mutuality?

SARAH: I think so—being in the fullness of that season of new life. I think that for a long time, I felt like you were more likely to be trying to bustle around and do other things rather than just sitting and being with Sage—and that felt really hard to me. Those tasks were potentially important and made our lives go more smoothly together. But I think it was largely an unspoken restlessness: that you were having a hard time sitting and being with Sage.

NATHAN: I think that's true. What I learned about myself is that when I am having a hard time, I tend to get really logistics-busy. It feels good to complete something concrete. Whereas just sitting in all the feelings of helplessness and confusion is really hard. And I know that's very much a conditioned male reaction: if I complete or fix something, that will make me feel better.

SARAH: I get that! I also have a drive these days to do finite tasks. It feels so good right now to move my body and complete a task.

Also, I sat with a lot of rising and falling feelings and memories, asking myself, "Wow, did I do everything that I wanted to do with my life before my life became intimately tied with this other human? I know his schedule and routine, and my life centers around him."

I don't think you shared that shift with me. You were still longing for a camping trip. I knew that wasn't going to happen for a while.

NATHAN: Part of that is that you spend more time with Sage, and you know his routines much more intimately than I do. I sometimes wonder if I were single parenting if I might still try to do something like go camping. Maybe that's just a difference in who we are and what we try. And it is also true that I sometimes get too ambitious.

SARAH: I want you to have space to experiment and learn things for yourself, and I also want you to respect my wisdom. I think I am still feeling unclear about what we do. What does equity look like in a time of imbalanced roles that are traditionally connected to patriarchy?

I feel like what I am asking from you is stillness and just being with me. I don't feel like that's so huge now, since Sage is so enjoyable to be with. You had a shift around the three-month period when you started to enjoy our time together.

NATHAN: It was so nice! I was so excited for that! I was starting to wonder when I would experience joy as a parent, and I was really thankful when I felt that joy!

SARAH: You were worried about it?

NATHAN: I was! I thought I loved kids.

SARAH: We thought you were the more nurturing one of the two of us!

I guess when I start to feel more concerned is when I hear other young folks socialized as women who are staying at home with children experiencing similar patterns. That's when I feel like it's actually not okay. A lot of people say things like "When my partner is home, he tries to do a bunch of stuff. The baby is in there whining in a way that I have a really hard time listening to, so I end up taking care of the baby, even though he is supposed to be doing it."

What's my work in that? If we share equitably, do I need to get used to hearing some sounds that I would normally be responding to? Or can I ask you to try to stop with the logistics and be with the baby, even though that is uncomfortable to you?

NATHAN: It's a question of what can and should we ask of each other.

It's helpful for me to hear you say, "This is a thing that comes up with a lot of people I've talked to." It helps me recognize another layer of patriarchy. Do I have to hear that other people are experiencing it before I believe you? Is that what's happening? Maybe! That feels terrible.

SARAH: It's hard to see how patterns play out in yourself, right? I can more intuitively say, "I think this is related to gender socialization" than you can.

NATHAN: Agreed. And I still struggle with, When is this just a difference in how we parent and when is it a gendered pattern? But you're right.

SARAH: Right now, I am thinking about how we do the work of building compassionate community, how caretaking people can feel the most supported, how unspoken things can become spoken, and how we do parenting intentionally.

NATHAN: I think the other piece of that conversation is the open question for myself: When do I need to pay attention to patriarchy patterns? When we frame it as me setting aside what I am doing and responding to baby cries as resisting patriarchy, I am much more willing to stop what I am doing and show up, because that matches what I value and want.

Final Thoughts from Nathan

This process of writing, talking, editing, and then reflecting some more on how we resist patriarchy in our parenting has been transformative for me. As a person socialized male, I realized through this process that one of the most important ways I can resist patriarchal gendered patterns is taking a deep dive into this conversation and then reading what I said in it.

There were times when I noticed behavior I hadn't seen before—like Sarah asking a question a few times before I finally answered it. There were also times when I would read Sarah sharing a difficult experience or vulnerably sharing a need, and I would think to myself, "Why didn't I stop right there and express empathy for her or ask her more about what that was like? Why did it take so much centering on myself and my own experience before I asked her about hers?"

It's hard to see myself in a negative light, but for me, that's part of the transformation. I have to notice what is already there before I can change into what I want to be. This process has helped me see that I want consistently to check in with Sarah about how patriarchy is showing up in our relationship.

And while Sage is not old enough for me to explain the way I am attempting to resist patriarchy, I know he will be increasingly watching how I parent—when I show up, how I show up, and how it relates to my parenting together with Sarah. Even beyond that, I want to be able to tell him when he's older how I attempted to navigate all this—flaws and all— and I hope it will help him do the same in his own context and generation.

Final Thoughts from Sarah

Our superpower as a couple is processing. We are constantly thinking about how systems are at play in our relationship and in the larger work we do in the community. I am grateful that

Nathan and I share the foundational values of reflection, honest sharing, and commitment to shifting when we need to.

For me, the transformational work of this conversation exists in the space between us and serves to illuminate the gritty details of incorporating children into movement space. It is a challenge for me to do deeper vision work and to be present in community space when I can't predict Sage's changing needs. I have had to get better at adapting, letting things go unfinished, and holding more openness and less control. When children are present, everyone is invited to be better at shifting the plan in the moment.

Feeling needs, finding language for them, then asking for help have been my biggest growing edges throughout this season. This is a wisdom skill that can only be strengthened through experience: learning when it is time to practice my own autonomy, when to roll with change, and when to not be afraid to call in support.

Undoing patriarchy is crucial in lifting up the radical work of raising the next generation and inviting the whole community into that call. The challenging negotiation within Nathan's and my relationship is a fractal of that larger transformation. Growing with a baby is a new passage into living more fully in a holy vision of messy, beautiful interdependence.

Reflection Questions

1 As I read about the places Nathan and Sarah named in their relationship where patriarchy showed up, what surprised me? What resonated with me?

2 As I think about my relationship(s), where do I most see patriarchy showing up? Are there ways I am already actively engaging the struggle?

3 Where are the places in my relationship(s) affected by patriarchy that I want to shift? What are the barriers to making a shift? And what would it take to move forward with that shift? How might it change my relationship(s) if I did?

9
Ableism

Opening Doors and Finding Transformation

Janice Fialka

Janice Fialka has been an activist for fifty years, married forty years, and parenting thirty years! Her experiences are rooted in a relentless pursuit to speak truth to power, to honor the dignity of each human being, and to intentionally build relationships and community. She loves shoveling snow and feeling the wind in her hair. Her professional roles include being a social worker, a founder of teen health centers in Michigan, the author of several books and articles, the maker of a film, and a nationally recognized presenter on topics related to disabilities and parenting a child with a disability. Her most precious identity is as the mother of Micah and Emma, both of whom are featured in her book *What Matters: Reflections on Disability, Community and Love* (Inclusion, 2016) and the documentary *Intelligent Lives* (directed by Dan Habib, 2019). To her surprise and delight, she has found her power in storytelling.

No one is truly prepared for parenting. I know I wasn't, especially when we learned that our son had disabilities. Those early years were frightening, unsettling, and at times lonely. But that's not the end of our story—not by any means. In our thirty-five years as Micah's parents, his father and I have stumbled our way into a few of the "great lessons," which are always guided by the question, What does it take to cultivate a meaningful, joyful, and inclusive life for our son, our family, and the community at large? I offer reflections and practical suggestions on some of those lessons: What kind of emotional support do families with children with disabilities want/ need? How can families that do not have children with disabilities connect with others that do? How do we have those uncomfortable conversations that lead to better communication and community? What does it take to advocate and challenge the often unspoken ableism that exists in our communities and schools—and in ourselves?

An Unfamiliar Dance

One night in 1988, unable to sleep, I took my familiar yellow pad of paper, huddled up in the corner of my couch, and wrote. I had a lot to say. Earlier that day, my husband, Rich, and I had participated in a difficult, life-changing meeting about our firstborn, four-year-old son, Micah. His neurologist, occupational therapist, physical therapist, speech therapist, and others had sat with us at an immense wooden table, the kind I imagine King Arthur and his knights would have gathered around to discuss the affairs of the kingdom.

We all knew Micah's development was delayed, but at this meeting, Rich and I formally learned that his was more than a temporary condition. His disabilities were significant and would be lifelong. We left the meeting, descended the clinic stairs, walked to our car, and sobbed.

We were stunned, terrified of his future—*our* future. We hardly knew how to raise a toddler, let alone one with disabilities. The babies of our friends pulled to standing, stacked blocks, pointed to the color red, threw balls. *Why didn't our son? What did I do to cause this?* I was invaded by so many disturbing thoughts—and, if I am honest, with some shame. Maybe the universe was telling me that I wasn't deserving of a "typical child."

At a time when we most needed others, we often felt alone. When we most needed people to ask us how we were, we were frequently met with silence. Friends and family didn't know what to say—nor did we. What words could we use to describe what we were learning about Micah, about ourselves?

I remember practicing in front of the mirror, awkwardly repeating words as if I were speaking a foreign language. "Yes, Micah is delayed. Yes, Micah gets therapy twice a week. Yes, Micah has special needs." I didn't want to say "cognitive and neurological impairment"—or the then commonly used "mental retardation"—with all the stigma these labels carried.

It is hard to admit all of this now, but I didn't always like what I was learning about myself. I had attacks of anger, terror, and guilt that overpowered me at times and kept me from seeking support. As much as Rich and I wanted and needed to feel connected to our friends and their children, it was hard to be with them. At birthday parties and on soccer fields, their kids were reminders of what we were not seeing in Micah.

Over time, we learned that it is not uncommon for families with children with disabilities to lose some friends, especially in the early years. We probably pushed some away with sharp words, giving mixed messages. "Ask us about Micah." "Don't ask us." "Tell us about your child." "Don't tell us!" We lived in the muck of fear and "Why me?"

Well-meaning people offered counsel that hurt more than helped. Some assured us that Micah would "grow out of it." We heard all too frequently about how "Albert Einstein didn't talk until he was four years old." Perhaps the most difficult was "God doesn't give you more than you can handle. Micah is lucky to have you two as parents." I wanted to shout, "I did not choose this! This is more than I can handle!"

Recently, at our local farmer's market, we ran into a friend whose son attended a play group with Micah thirty years ago. We shared a "great to see you" hug and reminisced. We gave updates on our families, lightly chatting.

Suddenly her mood shifted. She hesitated and then mentioned that she had purchased a copy of our book, *What Matters: Reflections on Disability, Community and Love*, which chronicles Micah's life over three decades. Her eyes welled with tears. She said that as she read the stories of our early years raising Micah, she remembered how awkward she felt as a friend to us and as a new parent to her son: "I didn't know what to say to you about Micah . . . and so I didn't say anything. I couldn't handle both your feelings and my fears. I worried, 'What if this happens to my family?'"

My husband and I were surprised and moved. We quickly offered reassuring nods and told her, "Those first years were hard for all of us." Now, years later, we finally had words and ways to understand her feelings and ours. Our parting hug was one of healing, hope, and a sense of greater ease about our past uneasiness.

We have learned by trial and error, tears and sleepless nights, that breaking the silence and having the difficult conversations are necessary to cultivate our compassion and connections with one another. Now people often seek our advice: "What should I do or say to parents whose kids have delays or disabilities?" I remind them that there is no one best way, though I find that honesty is a darn good way to begin. Say something like "I am guessing that you might be going through a lot right now. I'm not sure exactly what to say, but I want you to know I care about you and your family. Let me know if there is anything that I can do or say that would be helpful." All parents want their children to be given opportunities to have friends, and if parents of children without disabilities are uncertain or worried about how to include our children with disabilities, it is okay to ask us what's best.

Despite the troubling, uncertain times, on most days, we did not let our fears, awkwardness, or heavy emotions interfere with loving our son. We attended children's musical concerts, singing "Baby Beluga," "You Are My Sunshine," and "This Little Light of Mine." Our songs and silly dances carried into our kitchen, car rides, and bedtime rituals. We played and laughed—even if we had cried the night before.

We worked hard not to isolate ourselves from other families and their children. When Micah was toilet trained at the age of four, we had a party. Our friend dressed in a Mickey Mouse costume, bringing giggles and ice cream to Micah and a few neighborhood kids. Turns out we were not so alone.

Here's what's really important: we began to know our son for who he was. At times, we wished that things would be different, but he was a patient teacher and didn't give up on us! As tough as it is for me to revisit those early years with their fear, shame, and anger, I own that experience as a part of our journey. It was our beginning. It's how we started this unfamiliar, unexpected dance. It is how we were then—and most importantly, it is far from where we are now. Our beginning steps as Micah's parents were the beginning of our own transformation.

A Change of Doors

As we grew in our understanding of Micah and what he needed, our energy moved from surviving to settling into our life as parents. Going to the park wasn't always easy for me, but that's where kids were, and Micah needed to be there too. Swinging on swings could happen in many ways. If his legs couldn't pump, my gentle push released his sway and his delightful "Whee!" I began to take my cues from him. He was happy, so why not join him!

When Micah was four years old, it was time for preschool. Our friend Jeannine was the owner and teacher of Blossom, a small neighborhood preschool. Jeannine created a warm, loving atmosphere with her students in her cozy home. She acknowledged and celebrated differences. "Micah's way" of jumping, with his feet on the floor and his arms wiggling up in the air, was just another way to go up and down. She invited each child to jump "their way." She stretched my own thinking and deepened my understanding of what it means not just to be a kid but to be human: we don't all have to do things the same way, at the same time, in the same sequence.

As much as Jeannine respected Micah's ways, she also challenged him to try new things and take risks. In incremental steps, she coached him to climb on all fours across the high bar over the swing set, slowly weaning him of her hands-on support. With complete confidence, she cheered him on. "You can do this, Micah." Words meant for Micah and for me too, the terrified mom—words I needed on a regular basis. Micah's lifelong sense of self-confidence and drive were planted at Blossom. He belonged—and that early experience remains with him, in him.

When Micah was old enough to attend public school, he began in a self-contained special education class in a different part of the building from his same-age peers, separated from them during most classes. Midway through first grade, Micah said to us, "I wanna go in the same door with all my friends." We listened—with some reservations and uncertainty. Being in a classroom where he received "specialized" services was the common educational practice. How would we challenge this standard? We had no experience, no knowledge, and little support.

Both my husband and I had for years been activists involved in the peace, women's, antiracism, and LGBTQ movements. At the age of one month, Micah had attended his first peace march, nestled in a blue corduroy carrier held close to my heart. When he informed us that he wanted to be with his peers in the same classroom, we began to understand that Micah's disability was not a special education issue; it was a social justice issue. With the help of many experienced families, professionals, disability activists, and most importantly, Micah, we realized that he did not need fixing; he needed respect, understanding, and authentic support.

We took new questions into the movement community. How will we ever create a world of honoring differences if we keep children separated? Who's not at the table, in the room, in our neighborhoods? How do we stop segregating people with disabilities? What supports are necessary for their full inclusion? Shouldn't *all* mean *all*? Later we learned that this segregation and discrimination has a label too: ableism.

After a lot of research about inclusion of children with disabilities in schools, we advocated for Micah to be the first student in his school district with intellectual disabilities to be fully included in all general education classes, K–12, with supports. The door didn't open easily, but Micah was unwavering in his insistence that he belonged with his classmates. The first day he walked through the same door with them, his smile proved that this was the right entrance.

Micah's inclusion required a shift in thinking and practice among us, the school staff, and the community, which often felt overwhelming. We attended conferences and brought back resources, teaching strategies, and enthusiasm to Micah's school—which were not always welcomed. We sought out leaders and activists in the field who taught us, mentored us, and supported us to do what no one had done before in our community.

Though I found it frightening to make public comments and seek support, Rich and I learned that it was critically important to inform parents at school meetings that Micah was in their child's classes. We shared that we were excited for Micah to get to know their kids, we let them know that he has special needs and learns differently, we welcomed their support in including him in activities in and out of school, and we invited their questions. Most were hesitant to ask us anything, so we learned to initiate conversations and encourage playdates.

One wise teacher noticed one of her students regularly playing four square with Micah during recess. She encouraged the mother of that child to consider a playdate with Micah. That was all that was needed. Through the middle and high school years, Micah and Michael spent time together. When it was time for the high school prom, they shopped together for their tuxedos.

Another teacher admitted to me that, though she was excited about including Micah in her class, she worried about making mistakes. I was so pleased with her honesty, and I assured her that mistakes would happen but we could talk and work through the challenges together. Once again, breaking the silence and sharing our vulnerabilities helped create trust.

Stumbling became part of our dance. I'm sure at times Rich and I were seen as annoying or difficult. I recall one meeting when I noticed a teacher leaning slightly away from me, trying not to make eye contact. I had experienced this in other meetings, but this time I managed to pause and take a deep breath. To my surprise, I teared up. With not a lot of elegance,

I mumbled something like "I think you see me as angry." Some heads nodded ever so slightly. I explained that what I actually felt was fear—fear that Micah wouldn't get what he needed, fear that I was failing as his mother, fear that they might give up on him. The spirit in the room immediately shifted, and one teacher said, "Advocating for your child, being at a meeting with all of us around this table, isn't easy. Take your time." What a gift her understanding and validation were to me.

With the guidance of leading educators and inclusion specialists, we encouraged teachers to modify the curriculum for Micah. We practiced how to hold high expectations for his learning while creating reasonable accommodations based on his abilities. He did not have to learn all that his classmates were learning. Our goal was to help him learn what he could, followed by nudging to deepen or expand on his growing abilities.

Our meetings with the school team were sometimes uncomfortable and scary. "If Micah can't read or write in the typical way, how will he complete assignments?" In some cases, an audiotape recorder was the answer. In his high school class on the history of the Vietnam War, he worked with his paraprofessional and interviewed people who were involved in the antiwar movement, then submitted the audiotape as his "written" assignment. As technology advanced, so did Micah's ability to receive and share information. Using voice-to-text programs and a screen reader, he began to access information on his own. I will never forget the first email he sent me: "Hi mom. From Micah."

Now Micah is prolific in his almost-daily Facebook posts, like this one: "I'm having an amazing day. I did 25 pushups. I volunteered at Planned Parenthood today. Don't forget to vote today. Send me your favorite recipes." People across the country follow Micah, encouraged and empowered by his enthusiasm, his advocacy, and his quality of life.

Circles of Support

As we researched more about inclusion, we learned the need to create intentional opportunities for classmates to be together with students with disabilities, often called Circle of Friends or Circles of Support. We were intrigued by this approach, as we were becoming more aware that Micah's classmates were often friendly with him (for example, asking, "Hey, Micah, how are you doing?" as they passed him in the hallways) but were not playing with him during recess, eating with him at lunch, or hanging out after school.

When Micah was in third grade, we worked with his teacher and the school social worker to invite a few of his classmates to meet weekly in a group that included him. The emphasis of the Circle gatherings was on having fun and building relationships. The kids played games, ate treats, and sometimes talked about ways that Micah could be included in activities.

They periodically talked about challenging issues. For example, Micah often resorted to repeated poking and pushing at his classmates' arms to get their attention. Understandably, students frequently ignored him, gave him an irritated look, or moved quickly away from him. With respect, the social worker explained that Micah didn't always have the words or usual ways to communicate.

One of the kids was able to tell Micah that the finger poking bothered her. Quickly the social worker moved into a fun role-play, in which the kids were engaged in finding a way to help him. One classmate came up with the idea of a raised hand (like a stop sign) to remind him to stop poking and wait a minute to get their attention. All the kids made the sign, including Micah, resulting in giggles and a fun dance of hands.

Although the new hand gesture didn't work all the time, it worked some of the time. Most importantly, the students learned that it was okay to talk about difficult issues. And Micah learned that he and his Circle could find solutions together.

The Circle continued into high school. When its members noticed that Micah mainly hung out with the teachers at school dances, not his classmates, they gave him an "assignment," gently coaching him to dance with five girls. With some nudging and planning, he proudly completed his assignment. Micah's report to us when he returned home that night was "I did it! It was cool dancing with five girls for a while, but then I got back to the teachers."

In a radio interview a few years post–high school, one of the Circle students reflected, "The Circle started out as support for Micah, but over time, it became a support for all of us." A few years later, when this same young man in Micah's Circle became a teacher and noticed that a student with disabilities didn't have any close friends, he started a Circle for his student.

In 2010, when Micah was preparing to move 417 miles from our home in Michigan to Syracuse, New York (gulp!), he announced, "If I'm going to do okay in my new home, I need to have a new Circle in Syracuse." What started in third grade was clearly fundamental to his life as an adult. And it certainly helped my husband and me feel more confident about his move.

Today, when Micah speaks to parents and teachers across the country about inclusion and what youth need to have a good life, he always tells them, "One of the best things you can do is start a Circle for your child or student." And then he adds, "Don't forget to serve pizza and have fun."

"You Just Never Know . . ."

After high school, Micah became part of the new wave of students with intellectual disabilities going to college, taking three classes each semester as a guest student. After four years, a new idea took hold as he watched his younger sister, Emma, move into her dorm. "If I lived in a dorm on campus," he observed, "I wouldn't have to take two buses to and from campus every day, and I get cable TV!"

The dorm door was the most complicated of all to open. But again, Micah was persistent. At the age of twenty-three, after a two-year-long "PhD" in advocacy, he made a bold decision to address the blatant discrimination and fight for his rights in a legal battle in the federal courts. It was a fight to belong, a feeling he had understood since his days at Blossom preschool. He sued the university, won, and moved into the dorm. The victory brought him into the national limelight, resulting in many public speaking engagements. It eventually landed him a position as a teaching assistant in the School of Education at Syracuse University, which was the reason for his move there in 2010.

Today Micah lives in an apartment with a roommate, has community supports, personal assistants, and his Circle. We still have flashes of worry, hits of humility, and spells of sleepless nights. But oh so much has changed since those early days—in profound, life-enriching, soul-stretching, joyful ways for Micah, for our family, and for the community at large. But as a society, we still have a long way to go. As I write this in 2019, only 17 percent of students with intellectual disabilities are included in classrooms for at least 80 percent of the day. But I believe a new era is evolving, one in which disability is beginning to be understood not as a *deficiency* but as a *difference*, not as an *illness* but as an *identity*. As Micah now says, "I'm not embarrassed that I have a disability; it is part of who I am."

Guiding Principles

As I look back over the years, I recognize several principles that guided our family:

- Acknowledge *all* feelings.
  When I review the range of feelings available to humans, I am confident that I have experienced most of them as a mother, often unexpectedly and mostly more than one at a time. Finding friends and family who listen with compassion and kindness—who do not rush in with advice or a fix-it fallacy—has been essential to my survival. They have allowed me to move beyond strong emotions, toward clarity, and a few steps beyond.

- Support great expectations.

"Support great expectations" is a common chorus in the world of disabilities. We had to believe Micah could learn and do more than what was often expected of him. "He can do more" became our family chant, not in a way that unduly pressured him (we hoped), but in a way that bolstered his confidence to achieve his potential and not be limited by current cultural boxes or labels. We learned that having great expectations requires the right supports, a little bit of nudging to get Micah out of his comfort zone, and making time for regular opportunities to reflect with Micah and his team on how things were going. Micah's capacity and vision for himself have grown exponentially because of these practices.

- Be mindful of changing parental roles.

A wise sociologist once told me that parents assume two roles throughout their years of parenting: *protector* and *guide*. The role of protector is deeply entrenched for parents of young children with disabilities, who learn early on to be fierce advocates. As Micah grew, Rich and I had to learn to step back and let him tell his story his way: hand in his not-perfect paper, sign his name with just an *M*, or not wear his boots in the deep winter months. The shift from protector to guide wasn't easy in our parenting dance. It required lots of reflection and conversation with our support Circle—and with Micah.

- Expect to live with uncertainty and risk.

I suspect that many parents of adult children with a disability have experienced an internal conversation that goes something like this: *Do I let him try new things? If I do, what if something goes wrong? What if he gets hurt? Would I have this same fear if he didn't have an intellectual disability? But he does, so what do I do?* I'm not sure this worried-parent script will ever cease, but after more than three decades, I am better at expecting these periods of anxiety. Eventually my husband and I began to take turns coaching each other not to let fear dominate our decision-making.

On my better days, I know that my mothering is not really about "letting go" of Micah but rather about learning how to "hold on differently." Ultimately, if Rich and I resort to overprotection and the false belief that mistakes can be avoided, Micah will not grow in his confidence and competence. The quality of his life rests largely on his ability to try new things and make his own decisions—with the help of his friends and colleagues, his Circle, and his family.

- Fall in love with interdependence.
  Perhaps the most important lesson we have learned is that independence is a myth. I have discovered that if I am going to build my community, get better at "being human," and make a difference, I need to ask for help—not with apology, but with dignity, grace, and intention.

  Not long ago, Micah was flying from Chicago to Detroit by himself. Just before landing, the plane experienced very strong turbulence, and Micah's fear escalated with each swerve and bump. What he decided to do remains one of my most moving reminders of how best to live. He turned to the person sitting next to him and said, "I'm kinda nervous. Could I hold your hand?" And he did.

That's the kind of world I want to live in: one that values interdependence, connection, and vulnerability. When we invite support from others, we are telling them that they matter. I want to live in a world in which help is asked for and given freely without guilt, pity, or scorekeeping but with a generosity of spirit that comes with the knowledge that we need one another. Micah and the disability justice movement have been my greatest teachers.

- Live in hope.

  Throughout the early years, Rich and I often heard, "You two are in denial. Your child will never ___ [fill in the blank]." One time, in response, Rich paused, shook his head, and explained, "I'm not in denial. Not at all. I am in . . . hope!" His insightful comment has changed many lives—certainly mine. Thankfully, hope is where we have landed on most days in our dance.

Reflection Questions

1 How can I (or my family, school, community) begin to be more intentionally inclusive of others with disabilities? What do I need to do, read, converse, or connect with?
2 What messages have I learned growing up that make it hard for me to say, "We're not sure how exactly to reach out but

we don't want to let this uncertainty stand in the way of connecting." What new messages can I create?

3 If I have a child with disabilities, what holds me back from reaching out to parents/families of children with and without disabilities? How can I address this awkwardness or fear? What do you need to strengthen your advocacy for your child with your family, school, and neighborhood?

4 Think about your community, school, neighborhood, and faith-based organizations. Who is not at the table? Who is not connected? How might I begin to include others who are not present or engaged?

5 When in your life have you risked breaking the silence? How did you feel, and what happened as a result?

10

Honoring Earth

Healing from the Carceral Mind and Climate Crisis with Joyful Interconnectedness

Michelle Martinez

Michelle Martinez was born in the Latinx diaspora of Detroit. She is a climate justice organizer fighting for the survival of Black and Brown people. Since 2006, she has fought gross expansion of fossil fuels and the erosion of democracy, working to restore human rights and our integral connection to Earth, home, and hearth. She is the coordinator for the Michigan Environmental Justice Coalition.

In this chapter, I explore connections to Earth and the ways it teaches us what aspects of mothering are healing. I talk about Detroit, disinvestment, and the Latinx diaspora to illuminate the overreliance on policing and punishment as a form of misogyny and a root cause of the climate crisis. I offer some reflections on how we can hold the contradictions of violence and forgiveness and resist policing and punishment through lessons found in the soil. I end with simple instructions on self-love and joyful connectedness to all our relations as people who seek to repair our bodies and relationships with one another and our common Mother Earth.

The Identity of Mother

"*Ay mamita*," met with an exhale or a nod, a slumping of the spine.

It's something, if said by an elder, that is endearing. Like "You, young mother," or one who might mother, "I see you and understand that what is happening to you may be fraught." Even for a young Latinx person, being recognized as *mamita* means something, reminding you and recognizing you within a universal familial position. Fixed and flexible, you are connected to an invisible lineage of womenfolk. Dangerous, endangered womyn who struggle to be.

"*Ay mamita*" is me watching over you with care and feeling through your hardship within that struggle, with you.

Being kissed at and called "*mamacita*"—his lips puckered together, sucking air slowly, closing his eyes, smiling—jumps here to another station. It's a radio station on a black Chevy truck in the summer, an arm hanging out of a passenger window like a scrub, licking his lips at me while I push the stroller down the block in Southwest Detroit. This is the Latinx diaspora, the place that raised me, culturally and spiritually, just blocks from the Detroit River.

I wonder, *Does he have any idea what that means, what it is meant to mean? Does he care how it will impact the children who call me Mama or Mami?* My toddler slows her pace and watches him, watching me. On many days, I've been called "*mamacita*"—the slight understanding of my body, my skin, by the male gaze. It places the onus on womynfolk to be dignified or pander to the male ego and respond, either of which abdicates our bodies from our will, placing us solidly and unfairly within the virgin-whore dichotomy. These slights of language make us objects, dismembering our bodies from the universal family. As I write, it's Mother's Day, on week eight or nine of the COVID-19 crisis in the United States. My mind lingers and toils in objectifying moments of my younger years. *This* is where unraveling began, where the "climate crisis" began.

The "climate crisis" did not begin with industrialization. It began with the manic control of living things and the movement of peoples. It began when someone looked upon life and wished to brandish dominion over it. It began when that gaze morally denied the life-giving power he could not control but sought to. It is perpetuated in the carceral mind, which punishes and harms that which he cannot tame. And now my daughter, eating a Dum Dum in her pink sneakers, is watching him, watching me, transforming me from Mama to *Mamacita*, as if this whole thing was absolutely and utterly normal—even causal. Climate change is merely a fractal of misogyny.

That black Chevy sat in front of old Bob Rodriguez's crumbling home pretty much all summer. The thing you need to know about Bob is that he was a fiercely hateful man, a one-man vigilante. His white, pallid skin sunk down and sagged on his bones. He cursed in spiteful ways at everyone who walked past his house, muttering under his breath. He dug in the trash at night for food for himself and his dog. Bob was my mother's neighbor and spent hours on his porch watching his exceptionally tall German shepherd, only three inches scant and three brain cells short of pouncing over the chain-link fence, run in circles, devastating his grass and all living things who entered.

Bob died alone in his house. His possessions were strewn all up and down the street: dozens of empty food boxes, nonworking appliances, two chairs with broken legs and torn upholstery. Two toilets were left in the yard, the ceramic cracked, either from when the contractors in the black Chevy threw them out the door or from before. How long had it been before anyone knew Bob had passed on?

The house's new tenant—tattoos donning his face, arms, chest, and legs—let my mom know that Bob's dog ate his body. The new tenant wears black jean shorts and large white T-shirts. I've never looked too closely at his tattoos to identify the images blotted on his white skin. He likes my mom and talks to her while drinking Monster Energy drinks from the corner store. My mom, she listens—holding her arms across her body and looking up at the clouds. She's careful not to look at him but is still and patient and generous with the minutes it takes to open the gate to enter or exit her home and hear his words. Last week, he left her a bag of green apples hanging from the bar of her white wrought-iron fence.

I called my mom "Mama" when I was a small child. She called her mom "Mumma," before she lost her at ten years old. And now, my six-year-old has started calling me "Mom," not "Mama" anymore, except at night, when she is in need of comfort. When the transition happened, I don't know; what lives there in the strange place between Mama, Mom, *Mamita*, and *Mamacita*, I don't know. They are indisputably distinct. The feelings of being called them are different, and on one side is one piece and on the other, another. *The true identity of* mother *lives within the in between*—pieces soldered together within the gendered body.

Whatever remains from our understanding of forgiveness and nourishment, mercy, lives there.

My mother, upon reading this piece, said, "I never got to the place of calling my mumma 'Mom.'" All eight of her siblings still call their mother "Mumma."

Mother Earth holds the key to forgiveness and unconditional love, outside gendered binaries, and punishment or shame. Earth is the place where fecundity, nourishment, and healing flourish, held by Indigenous knowledges and sacred becomings. To disrupt this pattern, the perpetual and surreptitious acts of the carceral mind must be replaced with nourishing care, sustenance of Earth, whose secrets hide under lawns and sidewalks and concrete cages and false dichotomies. I know our work parenting, mothering, is to reclaim and embody love and forgiveness, to bring voice to the invisible healing of that severance, to struggle against the patterns of severance from ourselves to Mother Earth.

Resisting Sacrifice Zones

There is a feeling of powerlessness when you are being poisoned in your own home. Knowing that each breath is a strike of the death knell—counting the seconds and moments of your own mortality. It's as if the moment you become aware of your own mortality, you begin to see, just on the distant horizon the terminal finish line moving closer and closer each day. Though its essence remains unchanged, each breath pulls you closer. The air pollution in Detroit has taken years of life from the community by way of cancer, heart attack, premature birth.

People of this land have toiled in the heat of steel factories, making love to the train whistle's lullaby, tilling soil and reminiscing on factory lines to the beat of the stamping plant, repainting and painting their homes with mixed matte yellow paint cans on sale off Michigan Avenue. Dancing in living rooms and showering in small steamy bathrooms while boys holler from street corners, while streetlight symphonies flicker and power lines threaten to fall with each stormy wind.

The dangerous little lies you told your daddy and uncovered with your *tia* with the first cup of coffee and the first honest question you were ever asked: Who are you? Who would tell you where babies and gasoline come from? And where the shit goes when you flush the toilet? Detroit is the Motor City, built on steel and grit and a dream that forced us to become in its toxic essence. The shadow side, the oily underbelly, is the cost of life.

Risk analysis describes the equation by which we define the extent to which we, as a society, take on the risk of dying in order to produce oil and gas. The state upholds a legal definition, an administrative process, and a scientific determination for what threshold of risk to our homes and our lives is acceptable in the name of and for the sake of American prosperity. If you live in Detroit, you definitively take that risk into your body through air pollution. Whether you live next to the oil refinery; adjacent to the steel manufacturers, the producers of automobiles that need oil, or the highways where they drive and spout diesel; by the river where its sludge is deposited; or amid the rotting infrastructure abandoned to maintain its profitability—you breathe sulfur and nitrous oxides and particulate matter, could be drinking arsenic and lead. As a result, you may lose your baby to premature birth, you may lose your grandparent to heart disease. Your body may be, your child may be, your dance may be cut short, harbored inside the acceptable-threshold-of-risk category, monetized in one-part-per-million numeration. For this reason, Detroit has been deemed a sacrifice zone.

Risk analysis is a fractal of policing. If we say that it is acceptable to kill a portion of our society so that we can drive—that logic must be policed. Society must accept, science must defend, and the state must administer the logic that we kill majority Black and Brown bodies for progress. If you are in the business of refuting that—like climate justice activists, like those at Standing Rock—you will be admonished. And because we are living every day under the logic that argues our lives do not matter, we must struggle, and resist, and love in spite of this poison. The onus is on us to dispute our sacrifice and prove our innocence by loving ourselves, our bodies, and protect our joy, our futures.

Detroit is an emblem of the survival paradox: loving in the poison we live. We live in the space between, the hiatus between where we once were—as people connected to our Mother Earth, intimately, inexorably—and something else. The inhabitation of that severance requires loving yourself in the negative spaces. It requires interrupting the normalcy of destruction to build ourselves, our romances and memories, our customs and rituals, in the liminal space of this risk. Love *mamacita* to reclaim our bodies and say yes to life.

Our memories live in the alleys and streets, in the walls and trees. Detroit, acquiescent to the arts of our own becoming, weaves the tendrils of an unspoken love for the awkward coming-of-age in the shadows of smokestacks and in alley-ways. Where your best friend is a ho and your mentor a hack, but you fully loved each firework, barbecue, and slutwalk while your heart struggles to beat. These are the imaginaries of the poisoned, the invisibilized, the displaced, who suffer to breathe through prayers at Sunday mass, in dialysis, and emergency rooms.

We are creating new imaginaries for the survival of humanity wrought through the lived pain and suffering of accelerated destruction, by and through climate disaster, the final shape of colonial violence. And as such, we are the struggling resistance to its final blow: the decimation of our joy.

Centering Joy and Love
for the Planet We Call "Mama"

Environmental justice lives in the moments we allow the land to sing and hold and rock her own in the smallest, most invis-ible moments—without the terminal interruptions of the state or normalized toxicity of its social order. Like the infinitesimal moments of nurture borne in the quiet morning to a peaceful child, having slept throughout the dark night.

In the summer, my children were taught to wash the dog. Fill one bucket with soapy water and fill another bucket with clean water. Don't spray the dog with the hose, he doesn't like that. Dip a small rag into the water and wash his fur—under his chest, on his back, and each of his legs. Don't get the soap in his eyes and try not to get water inside of his ears. Don't pull his tail.

Our dog, now seven years old, was the first baby of the house and prefers not to bathe. He cowers in the water when the children wash him. He tucks his tail under and presses his ears to his head. He tries desperately to remove his leash and bound for the gate. As soon as his bath is done, we take off his leash and say, "Go, Ooni, go!" And he runs around and around the yard. The children scream and jubilate, they jump and laugh as he rubs his face and his body in the dirt. The dog can't get dirty quick enough. The children are covered in soap and mud and dog hair and love the dog.

We tell stories about the dog and imagine what he does at home when we are not there. There are so many pleasures. He loves to wear the kids' roller skates and tumble down the stairs. He also likes to catch a ride with the man who drives the ice cream truck, because the ice cream truck man is a dog with a human suit on. Ooni also makes pancakes using dog food instead of chocolate chips and watches YouTube videos of other dogs dancing in tutus.

The children see our pet as a part of the family. My older child has taken to letting the dog sleep in her bed, petting him while we read stories each night. My children find joy in this care, and it is a choice that they make each day. Unprompted, they feed and cuddle him. And I tell them, he too will be laid in the ground, as everything goes back into the earth. Our joy is connected to his, like all the living beings around us.

In the spring, we have long, leisurely picnics. The children get to choose whatever foods they like, and invariably, it's some form of wheat and cheese, with chips and sugar. They choose the blanket and the plates and bring all of that to a spot outside as early in spring as we can—when the soil is still damp but not cold-inducing. The sun feels warm after the long, dark, sunless winter. We look at clouds together and talk about how beautiful the day is.

We play outside and garden, working in the soil together. My mother joins us occasionally, wearing her broad hat, digging and playing. She hunches her shoulders and chases the toddlers around the house, pretending to lose in each race. We pick up bugs and talk about them, and she pretends to be scared. The roly-polies are trilobites that lived before the dinosaurs. I tell the children the big, juicy grubs are bird chicken nuggets and special treats for the robins and they should leave them on the sidewalk. And the earthworms are there to heal the soil and they should let them hang with their friends. We plant seeds together in small amounts until they get bored and run away while I continue to labor, like my father who works the land like prayer. My body becomes sore, and as I rest, I think of its healing and strengthening in concert with the soils beneath.

I show my older child which plants to eat—because my younger eats anything at age three. Purslane, lamb's-quarters, dandelions, purple dead nettle. I tell them that the plants breathe and take care of us. I let them know that trees are silent and ask us to be the same so we can hear them talking. If you listen closely to the trees, they tell us to be calm.

We turn the compost, and I tell them everything goes back to the earth. Even us—even me one day too, yes. When the plants are producing, we put on our boots and collect the grapevine and Japanese beetles in soapy water, because they decimate the raspberries. I show my children the seeds in the watermelon and cantaloupe and how we save them. The foods they eat are few now, but the underpinnings of how we cultivate are there: how we survive and what we can do to reciprocate a loving relationship with the earth by knowing each of her great beings.

We drive to state forests and walk the paths, and I say, "Look up at the magical winds that make the trees dance." And we run and find joy in a space. We are trying to build a centripetal force for a center of gravity, wherever we are. Joy—because they deserve to understand what it feels like. As a mother, it's a struggle.

In the teachings of Christianity, I never learned what happened to Mary, the mother of Jesus, after she witnessed him being crucified, an unspeakable murder by the state. That powerlessness of witnessing that which you love perish by violence before you. But what after? Did she curl into a ball and writhe, weeping in darkness? Did she become an abolitionist and fight capital punishment? Did she pray in private or in public and exalt his death? I can't imagine. What does *mother* do when hapticality arrives—when the feel of what is to come arrives?

Climate change is here. Coronavirus is here. Ecosystems perish before us; the momentum of climate catastrophe and collapse accelerates. We are witnessing our beloved creation perish at the hands of the state because of the controlling and carceral mind. Yet the lessons of mothering, caring, tending, nurturing, healing, cultivating a future—in spite of this decreation—are in the land. These stories are in one another, as though they were the same being, together always: *mami, mama, mamita, mumma, mom* are one singular breath. We must practice and share, live within the paradox of becoming what has been lost, fight for love and justice. We must create and re-create, forge ourselves together into a semblance of mothering, offering love and protection and care for our children—and for the planet that we call "Mama."

Reflection Questions

1 How do I disentangle the legacy of industrialization from my identities and reclaim my connection to the earth? Where do I see the severing of humanity from a common mother, defining of human exceptionalism, and settling onto the land as a form of domination? What are the forms of domination of the human body, and how do they extend to and access forms of spatial and cultural domination over the earth?

2 What is the process of reconnecting to prior and bodily knowledges that support decolonization? How can exploring and interrogating the space between the present arrangement and the future we want contribute to positively reconfiguring our social relations and (improbable as it may feel) to achieving real justice?

3 How can I engage in the beautiful struggle, with my children and my memories and my prayers, to hear the knowledge of my ancestors on Indigenous lands?

11

The Power of Story

Subversive Lessons from Grandmother Oak

Randy Woodley

Randy Woodley is a Keetoowah Cherokee (legal descendant) teacher, poet, activist, former pastor, missiologist, distinguished speaker, and historian. He was ordained to the ministry through the American Baptist Churches. Randy's PhD is in Intercultural Studies from Asbury Seminary in Wilmore, Kentucky. His books include *Decolonizing Evangelicalism: An 11:59 p.m. Conversation* (Wipf & Stock, 2020), *The Harmony Tree: A Story of Healing and Community* (Friesens, 2016), *Shalom and the Community of Creation: An Indigenous Vision* (Eerdmans, 2012), and *Living in Color: Embracing God's Passion for Ethnic Diversity* (IVP, 2004). Randy and his wife, Edith, co-sustain Eloheh Indigenous Center for Earth Justice, where they teach and learn and operate Eloheh Farm and Seeds.

Children know better than adults how to find themselves in a story. After all, their world is not complicated by work responsibilities, political turmoil, or planning for the future. What children have, serving as a primary motivator in their lives, is story. Whether pirates, princesses, or superheroes, we leave their imaginations intact to wonder at all that can be. The following chapter explores some of my own storytelling through a trilogy of children's books. They intersect childlike imaginations with the history and future of their nation and their own well-being. My hope is that my stories will one day help them and their imaginations, repair the historic wrongs done in our nation, view the cultural other with equality, and empower them to preserve the earth for future generations.

Garnering Wisdom

Having lived lives dedicated to serving our fellow human beings in the nonprofit sector for more than thirty years has been both a joy and a sacrifice for my wife and me. When we began, we could not have seen the toll it would take on our four children. Our life has not been easy. It has been marked by tragedies beyond what many couples suffer. As a result—which probably should not have been a surprise—our children have suffered emotionally as well.

We have seen some of our children go through forms of hell that any parent would have given all they had to avoid. I mention this now because they are, for the most part, on the other side of these tragedies and recovering. But I know this is not always assured, and in that, we are very fortunate. The particular stories of my children are for them to tell as they see fit. How we as parents responded and what we have learned is ours. It is from this place of being a parent who has seen his children suffer and come through it and having garnered wisdom through those experiences that I write.

I am a Native American legal descendant and my wife is a Native American tribal member. For years, we operated a Native American community, farm, job empowerment, and cultural center that served as a living school of sorts. The fifty-five-acre farm we called Eloheh Village was a paradise for my children, especially the two younger boys. They ran in the fields and played in the woods and at our creek all day long.

But after having spent years developing a holistic approach to healing our Native American communities, my wife and I lost everything. We lost it due to violent pressure from a white supremacist paramilitary group, whose members fired a .50-caliber machine gun on our property line, day and night. This was not the first time we felt resistance, and even persecution, because we are Native Americans, but it was the incident that changed our lives forever. Losing our farm and our means of support was the cause of years of pain and grief for me and my family.

When a parent faces insurmountable odds with seemingly little hope, there is no prescription for how to respond. At least, I have yet to find it if there is. But one thing that does seem to have stood the test of time is story. In story, we are granted the imagined circumstances of finding ourselves anew and garnering more options than we had before. One of the ways I have parented is through story, both reading to my kids and writing for them.

Some of my children now have children of their own, and I have four grandchildren. Something unexplainable but wonderful happens to us when we become grandparents. I've discussed the phenomenon with many other grandparents. The feeling is verifiable, and yet inexplicable. When we are able to view for the first time the third generation of a part of ourselves, following us, the feelings run deep. I would even say they are primordial. This sense is different from what we felt when we had our own children—still both joyous and solemn at once but difficult to put into words.

I write to and for my grandchildren and for yours. I write children's stories that are meant both for them and for their parents. I write for those who, through their stories and in teaching their children, want to gain the wisdom needed to produce the foresight necessary to pass it down to the next generation, so that they can add in some small way better experiences to the lives their young ones have ahead of them.

I want to share my experience of how three stories have come alive for me. I want to explore where they came from and my hopes for transformation upon hearing them. I offer them here in hopes that they will move within you and that you can claim your own power of storytelling.

I wrote the Harmony Tree trilogy as much for parents as for children. In fact, I've often described the series as "children's books, written to guide you through your adulthood." Even though children ages six through eleven will understand much about the stories, my intention in writing the series has always been for the adult reader/parent to take the child much deeper into the themes, expanding upon the stories at any point. Specifically, I reflect on five themes: animating nature, caring for the earth, repairing host and settler people relations, empowering women, and accepting people who are "different."

The inspiration for the trilogy comes from a three-hundred-year-old oak tree on top of a hill that was the only virgin tree left standing when loggers cleared the farm that became our home. I was always grateful that they left it for us to enjoy. That one grandmother oak tree, left uncut, offers some hope for everyone.

Restored Harmony

The first book in the trilogy, *The Harmony Tree: A Story of Healing and Community*, begins with the words "Not long ago, there lived a vast grove of ancient trees." We see a forest of virgin oak trees and what I refer to as the "community of creation," living together in balance and harmony. I take the reader back to a time when every living being in our natural ecosystem lived well together. I am not trying to establish any sort of utopian existence in the reader's mind; I am merely attempting to find a way to help children understand that, at one time in America, there was an ecological normalcy that depended not on destroying nature but rather on cooperating with it.

I mention several animals and birds that are either extinct or in danger of extinction. Unless we change the ways we interact with nature, our children will think of the snow leopard, the white rhino, the Siberian tiger, giraffes, elephants, and the rest of the endangered 50 percent of all mammals on Earth in the same way we now think of the woolly mammoth and the dinosaurs.

This vision of a restored harmony between humans and nature is a central theme of all three books. My hope is that children will learn to interact in a more personal relationship with nature. I want them to begin to understand themselves as part of the community of creation, not just, even in the best sense of the word, consumers of nature. I want them to wander in nature and wonder about everything they see, hear, smell, taste, and feel. But I hope they go beyond that and understand themselves not as intruders or tourists but as connected to everything around them and in relationship with it.

Historically, when Europeans first came to this country, one of their very first exports back to Europe was timber, largely from virgin oak forests. Europe's forests had been devastated by extreme overuse, which in turn affected the whole ecological system in very harmful ways. Large mammals were being decimated, and as a result, only the kings and the noble class were allowed to hunt them. Habitat for birds, fish, and other wildlife had been completely destroyed, which also added to the decline of healthy rivers and streams. In addition, the fisheries were all being depleted. How did this happen?

Europeans, having over centuries developed a keen and seemingly rational worldview, understood themselves as the masters of nature, not a part of it. In this highly developed dualistic worldview, which was likely first inherited from the Greeks, Europeans began to view the material world, including the earth and even their own bodies, as suspect. The mind, the spirit, and even their own laws and religious dogma became the ethereal measure of all things.

They cut down the forests, especially hardwoods such as oak, for their fortresses, churches, and castles. Hardwood was necessary in particular to make forges hot enough for the molding tools needed for these mass building projects, as well as for iron weaponry. The European worldview is one that leans toward competition more than cooperation, and there were plenty of wars requiring fortresses and weapons to keep the trees falling. That same worldview accompanied the Europeans who came to America.

The destruction of nature in the first book of the trilogy comes much later than it did in feudal Europe. Although it is described as sounding like "a thousand wounded bumblebees," the reader understands that the horrendous noise is that of chainsaws clear-cutting the once harmonious oak forest. The forest is decimated, and only a lone grandmother oak remains standing.

This utterly lonely and distressed grandmother oak questions her own existence as the last survivor of this genocide. Although she drops her acorns annually, hoping to repopulate the forest, when the young trees become of age, they too are cut down. Finally, grandmother oak stops producing acorns altogether. There is a sad pause here in the book, and rightly so. The sadness is meant to invoke thoughts of the trees as a metaphor and their ethnic representation.

Later in the book, it becomes apparent that the new trees being introduced are trees of a different sort. The keen reader will pick up the implication that the oak tree represents Native Americans and the other trees are European Americans. If they don't recognize it immediately, they have a more obvious hint in the book's final, double-page illustration of a modern Native American young man looking into the forest to see all his past Indigenous relatives.

The desperation of grandmother oak, her loneliness, and her loss of hope for future generations depict the struggle of Native Americans to this very day. The story builds on both the alienation of the other trees from grandmother oak and their own unnatural relationship with the land upon which they live. In spite of the differences and their ridicule, in an effort to try to help the new trees, grandmother oak asks them to "tell me the stories that connect you to this land."

The story being touched on here is one that makes most Western-oriented settler folk very nervous, and it creates cognitive dissonance. On one hand, most of the settler society in North America wants to do what is right by way of Indigenous people. On the other hand, there is too much at stake to deal with the tragedy of attempted genocide and stolen land, the story of which is a silent reminder that the issue will never go away despite how many generations pass. Not as long as there are First Nations left to remind us. The story—in fact, all three stories—is an honest approach to give parents reason to pass along a better one to their children. For one day, parents may need to answer to their children for leaving the story untold.

The happy final part of the story is that the new trees realize their stories are primarily not of this place, and finally they rely on grandmother oak to tell them the stories of the land so their own roots can grow stronger and they can heal. The conclusion of the story involves grandmother oak's healing as well. After years of hopelessness, her acorns once again begin to fall to the ground, planting seeds of new hope.

The particular lesson here is that only together as a community can we begin to heal, as is reflected in the book's subtitle. As Native Americans, who have lost so very much, we must realize that our path toward healing is not simply through our own empowerment but also through forgiving and living with the very people who are our colonizers—those who disrupted our families and our ecosystems.

Europeans must begin to understand their role as sort of "junior partners" in the relationship to Indigenous peoples when it comes to Earth wisdom and healing our community of creation. Euro-Americans, without often realizing it, contain the seed of destruction for both their relationship with Native Americans and with nature herself. That seed is the Western worldview. Only by hearing the stories of the land and wisdom from elders whose people have been on this land for many millennia will Euro-Americans begin to understand the world from a different perspective: one steeped in centuries of the notion that cooperation with nature, including cooperation with other humans, is better than competition.

All Things Being Equal

In the as-yet-unpublished sequel, *The Harmony Tree II: Spared by Fire*, I introduce people. That will hopefully cause readers to realize, if they didn't before, that there were no people in the first book. If that is so, I have been successful at humanizing nature.

The second book is centered on two main characters: Jade, a ten-year-old ethnically ambiguous girl, and an older, distinguished man who is referred to as The Chief. Jade comes to understand that the elderly man is not the sort of chief she imagined, but the fire chief of a Native American firefighting crew.

The chief of the tribe, she finds out to her amazement, is a woman. Jade is introduced to a firefighter who is a woman as well and who calls her favorite tree grandmother oak. In addition to the obvious theme of the destruction of nature through our modern forest fires, the second book also focuses on women's empowerment. I try to set up role models throughout the book that allow young girls to envision themselves in leadership positions.

The Ridge Creek fire, a fictitious forest fire but a scenario not difficult to imagine, temporarily displaces Jade and her family from their home, which is just down the street from a grove of oaks. When they are allowed back to their home, Jade wants to check on grandmother oak right away, and she also wants to thank the firefighters for saving their home and the grove of oak trees she loves so much.

Through a series of interactions with the Smoke-runners, the Native American fire crew, Jade learns more about forest fires, including the way Indigenous people controlled and prevented them in the past. Jade also learns much about Native Americans she did not know, including the fact that there are tribes living near her and that Native American leadership is equitable among genders. She also learns that Native American people have a good sense of humor.

These interactions are meant not just to teach child (and adult) readers a bit of what they may not know about Native

Americans. They also serve to humanize Indigenous people to a population with more than five hundred years of experience dehumanizing Native Americans through American myths, movies, and sports mascots. Hopefully, readers will have a different understanding of Native Americans by the time they finish the book.

Not only has the Indigenous wisdom of Earth-keeping been largely ignored by the dominant Euro-American society, but America's Indigene have been largely erased from history—especially any history that reveals Native Americans as more than the noble savage vanishing into the sunset or the pitiful, perhaps drunk, child-like creature waiting to be rescued by the parochial colonizer. By humanizing modern Native Americans as people who live in the same modern world as Jade, I hope to undo some of the old stereotypical notions. Jade approaches these issues with the curiosity, honesty, and humility of a child—the perfect example for us all.

It is important to the story that Jade is ethnically ambiguous in the illustrations. The colonizing strategy used in America—although having its roots in white supremacy, which is expressed most often through white normalcy and white privilege—has captured not just white people but people of color as well. Colonization is color-blind, and it is bigger than race. The Western colonial worldview has invaded all peoples.

One of the most diabolical strategies of Western settler-colonialism is the creation of self-hatred in those being colonized. Jade, for all we know, could even be an assimilated Native American girl whose family has long since discarded or forgotten its own history. She could be any other person of color whose people were forced to assimilate to white normalcy or who simply decided it was not worth the cost to resist colonization.

Along the theme of Jade being reintroduced to nature, to start a new kind of relationship with it, the fire chief gives her permission to talk to grandmother oak. As you might expect from a child before she is forced to lose her natural relationship with creation, Jade already has a love for grandmother oak. She has keenly observed both the human life (i.e., bird-watchers) and the bird and animal life surrounding the tree and the small forest. But Jade had never considered talking to grandmother oak. I think this level of brave and vulnerable action is the real first step in changing our ecological plight.

Sometimes even the staunchest environmental activists, with the best of intentions, are working from the same premise as those who seek to destroy the environment. For example, an environmentalist may love the forest and even risk everything to preserve the forest so future generations may enjoy it, but still the preservation efforts are for consumeristic pleasures. I firmly believe environmental activists are absolutely necessary for the survival of our human species, but does the premise need to be centered on human beings in order to have importance? Could it be that the trees, and the birds, and the four-leggeds, and the crawlers, and the swimmers all have a right to exist as part of this grand community of creation without us humans at the center—with all the other parts of creation being important in and of themselves?

I hope we can ask, Could it be that creation herself does not need us but allows us the privilege simply to be a part of the circle of beings? With that attitude in mind, I wonder if we might reintroduce ourselves to the trees and other beings around us by simply talking to them and expecting a reciprocal conversation—even though the dialogue may not take the form we are used to. In other words, not only should we be marching and taking actionable steps to save the community of creation, but we should also be talking to that community in our own backyards. A real and intimate relationship to everything around us is vital for harmonious living.

Because the second book is contemporary, it helps non-Indigenous people understand that American Indians are not myths of the past but are simply not on most people's radar. The story of contemporary First Nations involvement with everyday life protects young people from the spread of the vestiges of manifest destiny and gives them a new story to tell of the real live Native Americans who live their lives all around them. The story needn't be historical to have power.

Honoring Difference

At Native American events such as Pow Wows, it is not unusual to see people who "stick out" by the way they dance or don't dance, talk or don't talk. Labeling others "mentally disabled" or "autistic" is a way for the dominant culture to note the difference from its view of normalcy. Perhaps the cruelest form of notice comes when such people, especially in their young and formative years, are teased for being different and are made to think of themselves as "less than" those around them.

Traditionally, in many Native American societies, people who are mentally, socially, sexually, or physically different are viewed as those especially gifted by the Creator and are seen as very special, sacred people. In Native communities, the norm is not to separate such people from others or embarrass them because they don't fit in but rather to accept and even honor them.

Having a grandchild with autism has helped me return to our Indigenous values and to learn what it means to see the sacredness of his difference. I remember when our family was first told that he was probably autistic. All the worst thoughts of potential impediments to his future and the costs to those who love him went through my head. This pattern of colonial thinking and societal norms was already established in my own mind unconsciously. After some initial months of going through the stages of grief, I found acceptance by remembering the words and behaviors of my own Indigenous elders and teachers, by recollecting that each time in my past, when I didn't understand something, it had become a teachable moment. I now understand those moments as sacred wisdom.

The Harmony Tree: Different Is Good will be a prequel to the other two stories. It takes place in America, pre-European contact, and centers on a struggle that a preteen Native American boy, Sage, goes through while seeking to find his place in his tribal society. His serene friend and cousin Ja'x, who quietly accepts Sage's difference at every turn, is his constant companion. Sage's struggle takes place near an ancient oak forest, which he visits often. It is his special and secret place, especially the spot where he sits beneath the cool and dry shelter of one particular tree: a grandmother oak. Sage finds refuge in his conversations with grandmother oak and the whole of the community of creation surrounding her.

In many Native American societies, there is an inherent sacredness in young children, women, and elders. Men in such societies are the only group who must find their own sacred place.

In my tribal tradition, children are considered sacred because they come from the Great Mystery beyond, where Creator held them until their birth. Children are even considered teachers of a sort, until age seven. Women are considered sacred because they, like Mother Earth, give birth to new life. In many tribal groups, women are also generally considered stronger than men in many ways—but I wouldn't need to convince any woman who has gone through childbirth of that fact! Elders are sacred because they have lived so many years of life, garnering experience and knowledge and integrating it into wisdom. As they move closer to their eternal time with the Great Mystery, they are seen to gain more of Creator's wisdom.

Men, however—and, as in this case, young boys who are attempting to think about their own life direction when they become men—must prove themselves worthy. Throughout the book, Sage tries to find his place by attempting to become a great hunter and a great warrior. But his physical and mental/ emotional specialisms prevent him at each turn. In the surprise ending (no spoiler alerts here), Sage discovers that his own particular differences, and the wisdom he has gained over the years of sitting under grandmother oak, make him special and valuable to the tribe. Ja'x learns how to be a support to a friend in need.

If I could wave a wand and change the way society judges what is normal for the sake of my grandson, and for the sake of every child who feels they do not "fit in," I would do it in an instant. The third book is my attempt at waving that wand. I want children who read this book to think about those who are different from themselves and to be the keepers of a sacred trust: to not treat those who are different badly or allow anyone else to. But more than that, I especially want children who feel they are different to understand their difference as sacred and to discover their particular giftedness—and even their contribution to their own communities.

In the three decades my wife and I have spent serving the needs of so many different Indigenous peoples, we have, hopefully, listened to the elders and garnered enough knowledge and experience to formulate a few kernels of wisdom. I hope that each story that I have told and written contains kernels of this ancient wisdom.

In spite of all the hurt we have borne, in spite of the emotional and economic damage our family has suffered through the years, we continue to see beyond the tragic circumstances. We have learned to look for hope. Along the way, we have met so many good people who are wonderful and yet so different from us. They give us hope. Our children give us hope. And most of all, our grandchildren give us hope.

Because of the truth that children will gain through these three stories and the questions asked along the way by the parents, they will not forget them. In fact, the impact of story is so powerful that children will actually find themselves in a better, more honest place as they navigate these three stories and all the issues that they address. Isn't that what every parent hopes for their child: to face a better future by dealing with the issue of life honestly?

Our best hopes are found in the future of children, even to the next seven generations. I have found that only through looking back, perhaps through the wisdom of the prior seven generations, can we move forward with the wisdom needed. Only then will we come to realize that our own healing is tied to our stories coming together, becoming one grand story of hope.

Reflection Questions

1 How do stories play a role in my family? Who creates them? Who listens? What words do they weave? How am I honoring the stories my children tell?

2 What and who are represented in the images, stories, and authors of books in our house?

3 When have I seen the power of storytelling shift consciousness, lives, or systems of power?

Part 3

Reclaiming Community

Our goal is to create a beloved community and this will require a qualitative change in our souls, as well as a quantitative change in our lives.

—Martin Luther King Jr.,
"Nonviolence: The Only Road to Freedom"

I drag the card table out to the corner and lay out a tablecloth. I bring some extra old, cracked lawn chairs and scatter them about. It's Wednesday afternoon. Cedar and Isaac bring out cups and their change purse. I carry their cooler full of lemonade. This week we are selling kale, beets, garlic, and grapes. They all grew in our yard or down the street on some abandoned city lots. Cedar runs to collect the chicken eggs and see if there are enough to sell.

Our friend Luke brings over a box of freshly harvested tomatoes. "These are free," he says. "I've got too many and they need to be eaten soon." Estephany walks over with a cooler of *queso* to sell. Dawn brings over cut herbs. Oya stops to talk a while. Kathy and Mark trade in gossip. Another neighbor comes trading hot *pupusas* for a bag of grapes. Neighbors come and go. At six, I clear the table and take the kids inside for supper. But folks still linger on the sidewalk, letting the summer evening pass by.

Community. It is the greatest gift I can give my children. It can come in a million different forms and in every place. Community makes the load lighter, the work more joyful, and the need for standing together for justice inescapable. We need one another. This section delves into the questions of how we live humanly in relation to place and one another.

12

Building Community

Choosing Life in the Certainty of Death

Marcia Lee and en sawyer

Marcia Lee and en sawyer are cofounders of
Taproot Sanctuary, an urban retreat center
and intentional community focused on living
in right relationship with the earth and our
neighbors in Detroit. Through this community,
they are exploring and experimenting on how
to live a more integrated and interdependent
relationship with all of creation. En is a taiko
drummer, woodworker, artist, mushroom grower,
broom and spoon maker, and farmer. Marcia
is a Courage & Renewal retreat facilitator and
leadership coach; restorative justice specialist;
facilitator with PeoplesHub, an online movement
school; and co-madre for Healing by Choice!, a
collaboration of women of color doing healing
justice work in Detroit. Together, through the
love and power of their ancestors, spiritual
traditions, and community, they are committed
to living into the world we need for our children's
children and the rest of creation to thrive.

*We are expecting our second child to arrive soon! Our first passed in
a miscarriage. The miscarriage and what is happening in the world*

has forced us to ask what it means to become parents in these times. We have been forced to grapple with death in order to choose life. For us, this has only been possible through the power of community. Our lives are focused on building deep relationships with ancestors, neighbors, and the earth. With a baby coming, we are learning new ways to ask old questions about what it means to live a socially just and compassionate life. We share these reflections, written during the last months of our womb time, as imperfect offerings, with gratitude to you for journeying with us. I (Marcia) write in first person, and en writes in third, but our ideas are cowritten.

Sleepless Questions

It's 2:46 a.m. and I'm awake yet again. Before pregnancy, I never had trouble sleeping. Questions and doubts around bringing a child into this increasingly chaotic and volatile world swirl around in my head. For the sake of the earth and our community, is it even just to have children in these times? Though these questions still swirl, the reality is we have already chosen to become parents. So what actions do we take (or not take) that demonstrate our commitment to creating a socially just and compassionate world for our child and our community (human and nonhuman)? How do we stick to these commitments in the face of a culture that deals in death?

We are in a time of great turning. Not only are we facing the inevitability of physical death; we are also navigating times defined by a culture of racism, systemic oppression, destruction of other species, climate change, and more. Grace Lee Boggs, a visionary activist who lived in Detroit, Michigan, said this change is akin to the shift from hunter-gatherer culture to agriculture or agriculture to industry. We are now in a time in which technology is advancing beyond our capacity to move with nature's rhythms. Our economy is so dependent on dismembering critical connections that we have lost our way. As my friend Shakiyla Smith said to me, "The world is on fire." Those who already bear the brunt of human "wealth creation" are most impacted by this destructive fire. And yet within it, we are more connected across the globe than we have ever been before, people are rising up in creative and wise ways, and nature is taking back space. So how do we transform this destructive fire into a healing, restorative, and life-giving fire? And how do we learn from our children in this transformation?

For us, the answers to these questions begin with the land, our histories, and our ancestors' teachings. So we begin with acknowledgment, thanksgiving, and ask for forgiveness from the land and water on which we live and the people whose land we are on. This is the Indigenous land of the Anishinabek (Ojibwe, Odawa, Potawatomi), Haudenosaunee, Miami, and Peoria Nations. It is now a Black-majority city known as Detroit, Michigan. We are surrounded by the Great Lakes. Our people are immigrants/settlers/colonizers to this land.

En was born in Japan and grew up in Japan and Hawai'i. His mom is Japanese and his dad is white. His parents are Liliko and Mark. His grandparents are Hideko, Giichiro, Jean, and Richard. His immediate family lives in Japan. I was born in Iowa and have lived mostly in Michigan. My family is from

Taiwan. Although I lived there only briefly as a child, I also consider Taiwan my home. My mother is 高益夫 and my father is 李茂森. My grandparents are 高亮, 高馬玉英, 李清輝, and 李楊月. I grew up in mid-Michigan in a small, majority-white town surrounded by farms on Anishinaabe land. I was raised primarily Catholic with influences from Buddhism and local Taiwanese religions, and en was raised agnostic with connections to Buddhism and Shintoism. We both are cisgender, grew up with internalized racism, and experienced class privilege, including college educations.

I fell in love with Detroit and the people of Detroit during college. Detroit has been home for more than fifteen years. En came to Detroit to learn about nonviolence, moved here after meeting me, and then found out his paternal grandmother was born and raised in Detroit!

Beloved Community

Falling in love with Detroit led me into relationship with Grace Lee Boggs, who went on to become my mentor and chosen grandmother. Grace taught us the importance of (be)loved community—not at the expense of our identities but as people who struggle, learn, love, and grow together. To us, (be)loved community means to be-love for ourselves and one another. We cannot form a healthy "we" without first believing in and belonging to our own selves—not through perfection but by embracing spirit, body, and mind as it is and striving for deeper connection.

We have chosen a lifestyle in which relationship with the earth and our neighbors is more valued than relationship with capital and money. We essentially share one "job" that revolves around our home and community. Income is defined by worth for our community and not by the amount of money we make. We hope to create a soft landing space for our child, integral and integrated into our life rather than an addition squeezed into a preexisting mode. We know that not everyone has the capacity or privilege to live simply, yet we can all give attention to what we deeply care about, reflect on what we *really* need, and work together to determine how *we*, as a community, create access and sustainability for all of our needed resources.

We practice (be)loved community in our partnership. We believe that our journey as partners is an essential part of becoming parents. We both believe in community, compassion, love, social justice, living simply, and the importance of work and play within nature's rhythm. Our commitment to each other lovingly forces us to examine our contradictions and encounter the ways in which we perpetuate suffering in the world. We strive to be a loving mirror that reflects our highest possibility.

The nature of our partnership has shifted profoundly with the change of our family structure. We are learning to be a husband to a mother and a wife to a father while also exploring those new roles ourselves. The ability to diffuse tension, be patient with our own and each other's imperfections, and know when to address something and when to accept things as they are have been crucial to maintaining a tender relationship space for our baby. How we treat each other at home is how we treat others outside. Our partnership is our own 24-7 incubation lab to catalyze a more harmonious way of being.

Outside of our partnership, this womb time has also brought us into deeper (be)loved community with our wider circles. Through friends, and friends of friends, we have received almost everything we need for this child and have much to give away. Parents caring for parents is an incredibly subversive act, one into which we are now being welcomed. Our community has been amazingly generous with helping us clean, winterize our home, prepare food, do ceremony, and so much more.

As I have begun to get to know other mothers in womb time, I have observed that the more we offer other new mothers, the more they have given to us. In addition, my mother, 高益夫; my sister, Grace; and our close friend, Crystal, have been preparing food, teaching us about pregnancy and birthing, and helping us create a spiritually safe environment in our home. They will be with us after the baby arrives for the sitting month to support the transition (traditionally, in Taiwan, the motherbaby have a month of rest while the community takes care of them). Their gift of presence has allowed us to be present to these times. We hope to be able to pass on what we have been given to others.

We want to share several examples of community in our lives that intertwine home, work, and healing.

Taproot Sanctuary

Over the past few years, we have been turning our home into an invitation for community. We call it Taproot Sanctuary. The taproot is the first root for some plants, the one from which the others grow. Our hope is for Taproot to be a space for us to live in right relationship with the earth and our neighbors.

An important part of creating the world we want for our children is making sure there is space for rest, creativity, play, and possibility. It is a place where the sacred in the mundane is centered. In this space, neighbors help one another and generously share what we have. Making crafts, growing our own food, and using nature's grid as our main source of energy are prioritized. People often say they want to "get off the (human) grid." Instead of focusing on what we want to remove ourselves from, we focus on what we want to manifest: the power of the sun, wind, and water. By working together in this ever-evolving process, we create the vision we desire and expand our imagination for what is possible. It is easy to see how that vision will soon hold our laughing child, running through the herb garden and chasing the ducks.

Healing by Choice!

Another place of community is my work with Healing by Choice!, a women and gender nonconforming, people of color, healing justice collaboration in Detroit, started as a response to a need in our community. It has transformed into a call for activism to center mental, physical, spiritual, and systemic healing and to address historical trauma. As named by Cara Page and Kindred Southern Healing Justice Collective, "Healing justice . . . identifies how we can holistically respond to and intervene on generational trauma and violence, and to bring collective practices that can impact and transform the consequences of oppression on our bodies, hearts and minds."

If we do not transform ourselves and how we organize, how can we expect that what we are creating will look any different from what exists now? I am a co-madre with Adela Nieves Martinez. Our members decided that rather than "co-directors," co-madres is a more whole description of what we are. As those who hold the container, we are co-mothering ourselves and one another through healing. This work that feeds my soul also feeds the soul of my child—both through my physical body and through the ways that our community is coming together.

Diggit Detroit

Another project that breathes community into our lives is Diggit Detroit. It is a place where families of color work toward living on nature's grid and building beloved community by sharing vision, time, food, tools, skills, resources, and labor. We believe that reweaving the fabric of humanity through craft and agriculture is an unavoidable step to dismantling capitalism. We do "barn raisings" to support families with whatever they need. We intentionally center people of color to learn and share from the teachings of our ancestors. We center families because we believe that nonviolence starts at home. We collectively commit to moving from *dependence* on systems and structures that do not work for us, through the *independence* of caring for ourselves as individuals, and into *interdependence*, together creating abundance from one another's gifts.

Intergenerational Community

During this pregnancy, I have already felt that this child is deeply spiritually connected and cared for by the ancestors and our living community. The egg began to descend during the passing of my grandmother 高馬玉英, my mother's mother, and of Mama Lila Cabbil, a "water warrior" advocating for water rights in Detroit and a dear friend of Rosa Parks.

During our womb time, we have had ceremonies and gatherings for each of us and each of our babies. These ceremonies created space for us and our community to come together, create joy, and reflect on what we deeply care about. For the "blessing way" we had for Baby Mochi (the nickname we have for the baby because we have eaten so much mochi during this time!), we invited our friends and their friends over, shared food from our gardens, received blessings for the baby through our bodies, and invited those gathered to write prayers for the baby for us to have at their birth.

After this intergenerational gathering that spanned infants to elders, a friend's friend wrote us a letter. They said they had been feeling despondent about the state of the world, but participating in our ceremony gave them an experience of (be)loved community and hope for their future. Our collective soul expanded and took on new shapes and colors through ceremony, reflection, and commitment to growing our souls.

This is not easy work; we each struggle with wanting to be accepted and included: to "belong." However, the degree to which we work through childhood and ancestral beliefs and traumas is the degree to which we can be in loving and healthy community with others. We also trust community to be a part of healing. This healing comes more easily with a mindset/heartset of living in a communal way ourselves rather than expecting a specific person or group to always be there for us. Knowing that relationships change over time, we can bring a more generous, courageous, and vulnerable spirit toward others and ourselves.

Are We Ready?

Even with all the support and affirmation we are receiving, are we ready? I'm not sure. Life has been, and will always be, defined by death. And in these days when capitalism and white supremacy push an inhospitable, hostile system, destruction and suffering seem ever more present. At times I am fraught with fear and guilt about bringing another human into this world. But more and more, I am leaning into faith that this child's soul is choosing to be here now, that they can contribute more in these times by coming into the physical realm than not, and that I can trust in our (be)loved community to (imperfectly) commit to live the world our children need. As my body changes and this soul grows inside of me, I am also recognizing that the more I embrace that death will come, the more freely I can live daily in joy, love, generosity, and commitment to community and justice. As en reminds me, "The moment life begins, it also begins to die. And ultimately, life wants to live."

There are still many unknowns, big questions for reflection and discussion, and many ways in which we have already acted and will continue to act imperfectly. But for now, we are leaning into gratitude for this land, partnership, (be)loved community, our Creator, and ancestors; alternating between naps, eating, and walking; trusting that this child knows what they need; and that we will co-teach and co-learn with each stage and turn of this journey.

Perhaps community is how we choose life in the certainty of death. Perhaps as we heal, we heal others. As we parent, we are parented. As we give, we are given. Perhaps this is enough.

* * *

Addendum: We are happy to share that our daughter was born in our home in the first week of December 2019. She arrived after eight hours of labor, weighing seven pounds, seven ounces. As she began her womb journey during the death of matriarchs, she arrived in the physical realm on the death anniversary of her great-grandfather 高亮, my mother's father. She is surrounded by her ancestors. Her name came from our tai chi elders, her grandparents, and a ten-day silent meditation that we did while she was in the womb.

Reflection Questions

1 What does it mean for me to choose life in the face of death?

2 Who is my (be)loved community? What do I need in order to be supported and to cultivate my (be)loved community?

3 What are ways that I will choose to prioritize wealth of relationship over wealth of money within my family?

13
Risk and Resistance

The Cost and Gifts to Our Children

Bill Wylie-Kellermann

Bill Wylie-Kellermann is a nonviolent community activist, teacher, pastor, parent of two adult daughters, and grandfather to four children. He is the author of six books, most recently *Dying Well: The Resurrected Life of Jeanie Wylie-Kellermann* (Cass Community, 2018), which testifies to resurrection freedom as witnessed through the death and life of the partner with whom he shared the vocations of marriage and parenting. His other books include *Where the Water Goes Around: Beloved Detroit* (Cascade, 2017); *Principalities in Particular: A Practical Theology of the Powers That Be* (Fortress, 2017); and *Seasons of Faith and Conscience: Reflections of Liturgical Direct Action* (Orbis, 1991; Wipf & Stock, 2009). In Jesus, he bets his life on gospel nonviolence, good news to the poor, Word made flesh, and freedom from the power of death.

In living lives toward a world of justice and peace, what risks (small or large, alone or together) do we take? How do those risks and their consequences get shared by our children? Is it morally fair to them? Is it good parenting? Or even, perhaps, is that shared risk essential to how we learn and teach and love? From within the movements of nonviolent resistance, and even from within the Jesus movement called biblical faith, I have struggled with these questions myself. Let me tell you part of that story in two generations.

The Seriousness of Baptism

"**B**ut don't you need your dad's permission to go?" It was a joke line rooted in this father's fear. Her mother gone to God a few years prior, my daughter Lydia, a college senior, was attending a Michigan Peace Team training for a non-violent war-zone presence in the West Bank, Palestine. She would know the taste of tear gas and the high screech and body-rocking thud of sound bombs. In those days, the Israeli Defense Forces were forbidden use of live ammunition in the presence of internationals (a distinction practically without a difference), though settler snipers knew no such restriction. She would sleep some nights in a shepherd's cave and accompany young boys to their flocks beneath the illegal settlements occupying the hill above. In Bil'in, she would join a group of villagers trying to resist the wall under construction, which hemmed them in, cut them off from waters and their olive trees. Though nonviolent and creative, their efforts were met each week with the gas and bullets—regular casualties to be expected. My heart quickly took this measure.

To my question about a permission slip, Lydia replied, "You already gave me your permission. You baptized me." It was a stunning joke line in return, rooted in faith. One that we'd not so inadvertently taught.

Baptizing an infant in arms is a celebration that says to the child, "You are loved by God. You are surrounded with love and care. As a pure act of grace, you are already part of this beloved community and there's not a thing you can do about it either way. It just is. A gift. But here's the caveat: we now commend you to the way of discipleship, the path of risky and costly grace. Take up your cross and follow Jesus." Formula for bad parenting? Contradiction? Paradox?

One need not be a Christian to embrace this particular paradox. Folks of other faith traditions or even none at all must struggle with the tension of wanting children to know they are safe and loved but also raise them up with ethical values that challenge authority, with all the risks inherent. It is, however, the biblical tradition out of which our family and community lives. In 1986, Jeanie Wylie, my wife of beloved memory, expressed this paradox as a reluctance to baptize our daughter. In what has become something of an iconic article in our circle, she poured out her soul for the local Catholic Worker paper, *On the Edge*:

I didn't want to baptize Lydia.

My love for her took me off guard. I'd only been able to see her and touch her for a few hours and already I wanted the world for her. I studied her while she lay in my arms to eat and she stared back. I cried often. I was overwhelmed.

In a quick constrictive moment, I wanted to draw a circle in the dirt around Bill and Lydia and me. I envisioned a brick tower rising on the circle and securing us from intrusions which might not honor the bond of love and satisfaction that held us together. I never wanted her hurt. I cried when she cried. In the flush of raging feelings which came with the afterbirth, I became anxious and impatient if nothing could be done to calm my child. Having entertained the thought, "Even if she dies tomorrow it will all have been worth it, just to know her," I was terrified that she would die. Die, leaving a void like my father had when I was seventeen. Sacrificed on an altar to a God who routinely asks too much. I was simultaneously struck by the magnificence of what God could create and singularly disinterested in hearing the voice of that God again.

And then came the question of baptism. Water, words, community. Offering our child back to God . . . We would give her to a God who models the cross. We would invite her to listen for a voice calling in the night, to vigil, to put herself at risk, to leave family and friends, to speak clearly a truth for which one can be executed. We would thereby invite her into the risks we have already elected and, by God's grace, still will elect to take with our own lives. In the act of baptism we would wash away the possibility that our concern for her might justify a diminishing of our own obedience to our Lord's perverse ethic of vulnerability and gain through loss.

I know exactly what she was talking about. As parents we make decisions every day for how we engage justice. Where do we choose to live? Where do our kids go to school? How do we show up in the street when our community or others are under attack?

To stand on the side of justice often means that we have to take some risks. Some of these are modest. Others momentous. None are easy. They can be fraught with angst, uncertainty, second-guessing. We worry about our kids. But we also worry about what they will learn if we don't act.

These risks are made lighter when we face into them as community. Who helps us discern? Who holds us accountable? Who holds our children as we get dragged off to jail? It was community that made these workable options for us. Which is to say, it was community that finally made possible the decision to bring Lydia into the waters:

> Bill and I had discovered some areas where we felt particularly vulnerable to God—like our experience that the Bible makes very clear sense to us while in jail and our feeling that there is a (perverse) value in having to wonder if your house has been broken into or if everything you have accumulated has been burned to the ground. To insulate ourselves would be to shield ourselves from times and places where we have heard God's voice. It would make us less able to share with Lydia and to demonstrate to her the nature of our faith.
>
> So, we baptize her into the risks we've elected for our lives. We take her, in utero, to Nicaragua. We share with her this broken, violent world. We baptize her into the communion of saints who have been crucified in every

possible way. We baptize her into the grueling decisions at Gethsemane and into Easter hope. We lay her on the altar before a God who rejects our carefully laid plans and takes her life into His/Her own.

And in so doing, we smash an idol.

This child is no longer a reason to flee from the voice of God. Instead, we carry the child, with our hearts, toward the one who utters us and calls us into being. We claim our lives in that voice and entrust each other's to it. We loosen our hold, our desperate grip, on each other's presence and well-being . . . It is enough, it is more than enough to be loved by God. Our child is safe in covenant with our God who is neither predictable nor always comfortable, but she will find there a hand that wipes away her tears, an end to her thirst and a wind that sets her loose.

Call it a mother's prayer of letting go.

Is This Good Parenting?

The Nicaragua reference bears further mention. That trip preceded Jeanie's reflection and may indeed have prompted it in part. The two of us, or let's say three, were participants in a Witness for Peace delegation. Jeanie was toward the end of her second trimester. The "Contra war" funded by the United States against Nicaragua's Sandinista revolution was in full force.

Witness for Peace had begun a few years prior, in 1983, with a delegation of North American Christians to the contested campo war zone where the CIA-funded mercenaries were attacking campesinos to undermine the revolutionary process. When the delegation recognized that wherever they traveled, Contra activity lessened and backed off—perchance to avoid international incident with the *norteños*, or simply provide them less to witness and report—it dawned on them: What would happen if delegations were regular and constant? What if US citizens could hear the stories, document and report the atrocities, share the risks, and perhaps in the process mitigate, to whatever extent, the presence of violence? Witness for Peace was born.

I am a straight, cis, white, male, US citizen and a professional cleric Christian—a social location I bore in my person to Nicaragua. Apart from those afforded by patriarchy and clericism, Jeanie shared these privileged positions. We understood ourselves as deploying our privilege on behalf of campesinos. The thought was to turn the system of imperialism and racism back upon itself. This comes with questions that linger in my work to this day. Is using colonial white supremacy as a tactic of nonviolence not just problematic but a contradiction? It was therefore important to us that Witness for Peace took its lead from Nicaraguans on the ground.

Within Witness for Peace, such questions were alive and struggled over. International solidarity and street-level violation of national policy always remained essential tactics. And taking disarmed risks with one's life and health and safety was understood as fundamental to nonviolence as both a tactic and a way of life—even if in this case, we could return home after a few weeks. This we knew in our bones. To be sure, we were muddling through.

One of the nights in 1986, along with our delegation, the three of us danced together in a rooftop club overlooking Lake Managua. The moon was full. The memory vivid.

But when the moment came to consider the riskiest stretch of the trip, into the mountains where the Contra roamed and blocked roads, and we gathered to discern our readiness, Jeanie hesitated—but only briefly.

One of our number, Fr. Charlie Liteky, a Vietnam war chaplain who had returned his Medal of Honor in protest of the Contra war, explained why he was ready. I used to be able to quote him precisely by heart and wish I could now, but in essence, he said that he was baptized into Christ Jesus and so had already died. (This is Saint Paul's idea that, in baptism, we die with Christ so we are also raised with him into the freedom of resurrection.) Therefore, said Charlie, he was free to risk anything, including to face the trained terrorism, malice, and military hardware of the Contra. Baptism enabled his solidarity of risk.

Jeanie confessed in the circle that she was discerning for two. Though she'd thought to stay behind, she now felt called forward into the hills. She was baptized too. We both swallowed hard and gave in to the claim.

We were accompanying Juana Francesca, returning for the first time to her village of La Cruz de las Piedras (Stone cross) since her husband and two sons had been dragged from their home and brutally murdered there by the Contra. As we approached the one-room house, she began to shake and wail. While she grieved loudly and with all her might, we stood around, hapless gringos, hands awkwardly in our pockets, trying to take it deep into our hearts. Eventually, with a leafy branch as aspergillum, we scattered water around the site to reclaim it ritually from death. The water fell on Jeanie's brow, as on all of ours. Baptism renewal. Blessing and exorcism. Then we prayed, in two languages simultaneously, Jesus's Discipleship Prayer. Deliver us from evil.

Can you see how this might be backstory to Jeanie's mediation on baptism?

And then, as if bad parenting were never to be unlearned, or baptism ever to be foresworn, we did it all again four years later. This time the war zone was a trip to Palestine, the West Bank and Gaza, and the child was Lucy, Lydia's six-month-old younger sister.

It must have been spring of 1990. The Second Intifada (a largely nonviolent uprising) was in progress. We were to be part of an interfaith human rights coalition. It wasn't that we'd intended to bring a nursing infant along, but the timing was such that we couldn't leave her behind and so had resolved to make it work.

She actually functioned as a delegate herself on the entire trip, drawing the attention of our various hosts. Shopkeepers, mayors, and activists jiggled their keys for her and cooed. Children gathered around the baby to smile and touch. She flipped the ordinary script of Westerners coming to observe the camps or community center. She stole the show, winning over the holdouts, even hardline right-wing Jews. Though fully supportive of the Palestinian struggle, we met with everyone to share and argue views.

Once again, we'd expected that Lucy would stay back from the Gaza portion. It was already an "open air prison," though nothing like the bombed-out desolation of the present—camps we visited then have since been leveled to rubble. But she was adapting so well and Jeanie was so eager that we all pressed on through the checkpoints.

Late in that visit, we were chased down by the Israeli Defense Forces (IDF), our luggage searched and all the film taken from our cameras (except for that already hidden). At one conversation, we passed around the circle a tear gas canister marked "Made in Bethlehem, PA." At Jabaliya Camp we tasted its contents when shot, illegally, from the IDF guard tower at the camp's center. This represents a greater risk—in certain circumstances, even a fatal one—for infants. So we wasted no time in jumping into the van, peeling out, and covering her face with moistened towels from a plastic bag in our pack. Lucy is a person who remembers the day she was born, so I can't help wondering what all she was taking in. Once again, we were asking ourselves: Is this good parenting?

Why Is Daddy in Jail?

Before we left for our trip to Palestine, I had driven Lydia, a child of four, to stay with her Grandma Bea in Menominee. On the way back, down the beautiful single-lane roads of Michigan's Upper Peninsula, I switched on a tape recorder and tried to tell her in the simplest language why her parents were making this trip. In the unlikely event of a fatal disaster, I wanted her to have something to hear, a loving word in my own voice. The cassette still abides in her childhood chest of paintings, dolls, and books. I often wondered if she'd need to play it for a therapist someday.

Jeanie had done something similar in a different context, and it may have been she who gave me the idea for this taping. Our community had undertaken a series of direct actions at a Strategic Air Command base in Michigan. The B-52s there had been fitted with nuclear cruise missiles, rendering them precision first-strike weapons. I'd made several incursions onto the base, so my sentences were increasing, and I now faced sixty days in the Bay County Jail. I have friends and mentors who have done much longer federal bits while parenting, so in some sense, it seemed not that long a time. Still, Jeanie and Lydia came for some visits. These were so eagerly awaited and then so impossibly hard. Twenty minutes seated across a table with no touching allowed. Try explaining that to a three-year-old. It was excruciating for all of us. I believe Jeanie eventually left off trying to bring her, but that had its own problematics. So she created a cloth book with photographs of us and others of me with markered bars across the picture. It was called, *Why Is Daddy in Jail?* By no means was it *Nuclear War for a Child*, but it certainly was about planes and bombs that hurt people. It's also to be found in the childhood memory chest.

As our girls grew, taking them to direct actions or demonstrations was mostly part and parcel of kid care. During the Detroit Newspaper Strike in the nineties, they watched either Jeanie or me be arrested more than once in a series of blockades organized by our group, Readers United. There are great photos of Jeanie doing police liaison or press work with the girls clinging to her skirt. To be sure, these were very civil arrests, if anything implicitly orchestrated, not the sort where chaos can reign and people, even children, can be swept up in unforeseen risk.

The nineties marked a shift in location for the focus of our nonviolent direct action. Not that we ceased antiwar and anti-nuclearism actions, but we were bringing our nonviolence to bear more and more on local neighborhood and city issues. Antihandgun vigils and gun-show arrests. Anticrack marches. Eventually actions related to emergency management, the destruction of public education, and the Detroit water struggle. All these urban movements were led by women of color, often elders and veterans of the freedom struggle but also passionate young visionaries. Increasingly, we found ourselves submitting to the wisdom and brilliant leadership of Black and Brown women. In the process, we were forced to wrestle with our innards—the deep spiritual roots of white supremacy. And once again, it surely figured into parental and grandfatherly pedagogy.

The Freedom to Die

I want to say that in their tweens and teens, our daughters had increasing freedom to make their own choices about being in such situations. And it would be true; however, beginning in 1998, our life as a family and even community was heavily focused on Jeanie's seven-year illness, an aggressive malignancy in her brain. It was a tumor that normally takes you in six months. Her journey was a sequence of surgeries, alternative treatments, radiation, and finally the community hospice of her dying time. All that represented another engagement with the Power of Death, another access to the freedoms of baptism, and yet another set of lessons for all of us.

Even in illness and death, there are issues of resistance to be considered. Some risks go with the culture of radiation, petrochemicals, refineries, additives, hydrocarbons, air and water pollution. It's a given across the United States. But it's also a matter of neighborhood. Poor folks and people of color end up living, de facto or by design, in areas where pollutants are heaviest. Call it environmental injustice, even assault. With Black, Latino, and Arab neighbors in Southwest Detroit, we live adjacent to one of the most toxic zip codes in America: 48217. Driving over the long expressway bridge on I-75 south is to glimpse a landscape fit for a film on industrial apocalypse. The oncologists consistently waved off any suggestions of environmental causes for the tumor, but we often wondered if it was a consequence of the corporate and industrial contempt for Earth and human life.

At the same time, the work of healing and, when it comes to it, dying well in community are acts of resistance. Jeanie had determined to decline a number of the conventional treatments pressed upon her by the cancer industry. To the decisions about these and other healing matters, our girls were privy and often participants. They prayed and sang and laid hands on their mom, invented rituals, gave gratitude, traveled distances with her in pursuit of alternative therapies, sought out rest and beauty, wrote poetry, persevered in routines, stepped up to caregiving, and simply loved. Healing was a process to be lived, and they joined it fully.

As we've come to appreciate it, resisting the culture of death and denial means giving oneself full-heartedly to the work and grace of healing, and when the time comes, to the grace of dying well. Each is rooted in the same freedom. For us, the healing community morphed seamlessly into the hospice community. Jeanie had that freedom and commended it, before our eyes and to her children. Treatments and hospital trips ceased, but not love and prayers.

This is a genuine form of resistance. In our culture, death is underneath everything: from Indigenous genocide to chattel slavery, from Jim Crow to land theft and forced deportation, from sweatshops to oil wars, from industrial assaults on the planet to the threat of nuclear weapons. And so it is also aggressively hidden and denied. Death, however organic and literally natural, becomes a constant source of subliminal anxiety to be suppressed. In consequence, personal anxiety about dying ends up entailing subordination to the powers that be. To be fully free to die, as named biblically in baptism or resurrection, offers the fullest freedom to resist this anxiety. Is there a parental pedagogy for that?

Much the same holds with respect to grief. Culturally denying death, we also suppress grief and become inept at the rituals of mourning. Because as a family we resisted the funeral industry and retained control of Jeanie's body, the girls were able to not only fall on her and wail, keening their loss, but also gather themselves to help wash, dress, and prepare her for green burial. Yet another gift and freedom.

Jeanie's death in a hospice community reminded us of nothing so much as birth, specifically home birth. Being midwifed to the other side. In fact, these days there are both birth doulas (who help mothers and families through the emotional landscape of pregnancy and childbirth) and death doulas (who do the equivalent at the end of the life journey).

Full Circle

About the time Jeanie was writing about her baptism qualms, she was also speaking and doing workshops on "Birthing in the Face of a Dragon." The image is taken from the twelfth chapter of Revelation, where the "woman clothed with the sun" is pregnant and in travail of birth. In portent, she is pursued by a great dragon who crouches before her, ready to devour the newborn child. Though the infant is snatched up to God and the woman protected by an eagle and by Earth herself, the risk of birthing in the face of death is made plain. At the time, we would have named the impending threat of first-strike nuclear weapons to be the jaws of death threatening our newborns. Now we would be equally quick to name the imminent omnicide of cascading climate collapse, though the two are deeply tied spiritually. How do they give us pause, and to what do they (and all the risks in between) call us now?

Last spring Lydia and I had the opportunity to interview Joanna Macy, a student of Buddhism, systems theory, and Deep Ecology who at ninety is still commending active hope for Earth in the face of climate assault. I asked her what she had to say to young people hesitating to bring children into this present moment of history. She replied, "I'm grateful for those who choose mindfully, with clear understanding, to bear children into this time. Because we're going to need those newcomers coming in through the passage of collapsing society, carrying the grief, and moving forward into a life-sustaining culture that can be born of this."

Maybe it's not even ironic that Lydia is my editor in this reflection, that she summons the piece as part of a project on raising kids with a commitment to peace and justice.

A few months ago, in connection with the Poor People's Campaign: A National Call for Moral Revival, I did a twelve-day sentence for helping shut down the Department of Health and Human Services in connection with their complicity in the Flint water poisonings. It was one of six Michigan actions launching the campaign in the summer of 2018. Now Lucy and Lydia each have children of their own. We all currently live on the same Detroit block together. My grandchildren came to a vigil for prisoners during that jail time and were also there to greet me when I was sprung at six in the morning. They were well prepared for each event by a book that Lydia created for their bedtime reading: *Why Is Grandpa in Jail?*

To the vigil, the kids brought their own handmade signs. Lydia is good at providing materials and permitting them to say what they want. As I'm writing, the 2020 Democratic presidential candidates are here in Detroit for multiple debates. Union, environmental, and climate justice groups have staged a massive march to the site, demanding to "Make Detroit the Engine of the Green New Deal." I'm not sure exactly what Lydia's preparation was, but Isaac's sign said, "Stop Being President, Care for the Earth" and Cedar had a brightly colored, "I love (heart) eggs," which is true.

Just the fullness of the circle. I've had a hand and voice in the baptism of my grandchildren—into the Detroit River, no less. I don't underestimate the risks to which I'm summoning them, but neither could I begin to overestimate the beloved abundance of grace that is even now poured out upon them.

Reflection Questions

1 What are choices I have made in my life as a commitment to justice that make me worry about how they will affect my kids?

2 Are there risks I would be taking if not for my children? How do I reconcile that? Are there ways I should push through those fears for the sake of my kids?

3 Are there moments when I need to honor my children's courage and clarity, even if it terrifies me?

14

How Do I Heal the Future?

Reclaiming Traditional Ways for the Sake of Our Children

An Interview with Leona Brown by Laurel Dykstra

Leona Brown is a Gitxsan refugee mother of three from the Killer Whale Clan of the Fireweed House, living on the unceded, ancestral, and traditional territories of the Musqueam, Squamish, and Tsleil-Waututh Nations (Vancouver, British Columbia). Leona is a student and teacher of Indigenous plant traditions sharing her knowledge in schools and community groups.

I wanted to interview Leona Brown for this project because I admire her, and as an Indigenous person, she has a really different perspective from me on colonization, family, and what it means to raise kids for a better world. Leona teaches plant medicines at an environmental leadership camp that I started and both our teen daughters have attended. I interviewed her at the nə́ća?mat ct branch of the Vancouver Public Library—nə́ća?mat ct means "we are one."

Laurel Dykstra: *Connection to culture and traditional Indigenous medicines are really important to your parenting. Was this always true for you?*

Leona Brown: I think my journey started in 2013, when my youngest child, Jackson, was born. During my pregnancy, I took part in the Truth and Reconciliation Commission on Indian Residential Schools. I went to events and listened to elders speak.

My mom had already passed, so I didn't know much about her experiences or how many people were impacted by the schools. So when I actually sat and listened to their stories, that's when I learned the way that they were raised. My mom was really violent at times, and she was verbally abusive. Hearing the stories opened up this huge empathy in me, and I had a better understanding of why my mom behaved the way she did.

Yeah, for about one hundred years, the Canadian government, with the collaboration of churches, removed 150,000 Indigenous children from their families and communities and took them to residential schools. And the stated intention was "to kill the Indian in the child."

Going to parenting classes, I learned that in parenting, you do what you were taught. She was taught abuse and neglect—and some children were even killed. So that's all she knew coming out of residential school.

A lot of the people turned to drugs and alcohol to try to suppress that pain, but it only made things worse. My mom really delved into her alcohol when I was younger. I couldn't understand. "Why is she like this?" For the longest time, I actually thought my mom hated me.

My dad didn't want me when I was born, and I only saw him twice in my life before he passed away. So I felt a huge sense that I wasn't wanted anywhere. And when the Truth and Reconciliation Commission happened, it lifted a huge burden off of me. I said my prayers, and I gave my forgiveness to my mom, and I forgave my dad, and that made me feel better inside.

Dykstra: *So how do the ongoing effects of residential school impact your family and your parenting?*

Brown: From that point, I wanted to structure my life around my culture that was taken from us. Because nothing was taught to me or really handed down. My mom married into Gitxsan, so we were raised Gitxsan, but we never knew much. My grandparents were Nisga'a. So we knew we were Gitxsan and Nisga'a and we belonged to the Killer Whale clan—and that's it.

My whole life, I'm thinking, "How do I get my culture back? There's more to it; there can't just be singing, dancing, drumming, or being an artist." So I was trying to find my path. And asking, "How do I heal my family? How do I heal the future? How do I raise my kids in a way that my mom wasn't raised?" I wanted to break that cycle. I grew up thinking, "I'm never going to let my kids be treated this way. We're never going to starve, we're never going to be without money, we're always going to find a way—or I'll find a way for them. I'll never neglect them."

I had to process a lot of trauma. I'm realizing the trauma I had as a kid still affects me in my parenting. I find when something with the kids troubles me—if they're not moving fast enough, or they're being rotten to each other, normal kid stuff—it makes me break out and yell at them. And as soon as I get to that point, I hear my mom. I hear her voice coming out of me, and that scares me.

But I'm aware of it, and so I try to ask, "What is that?" That's my mom's parenting—how she treated me when I did certain things—coming out to my kids. So I'm trying to heal and do things differently. And I'm finding it has such a strong hold on me in my mind. It's really hard to let it go. It takes some really hard practice sometimes. Working with plants kind of forces me to be more gentle and respectful, so it helps me in my triggers.

Dykstra: *I know a little bit about this because when our daughters were at camp together, Maggie told me about her medicines, but can you talk about how your healing work influences your kids and your parenting?*

Brown: Well, my mom taught us food culture, but we never knew anything else about our tradition. So my journey with medicines started about when Jackson was born. I had gallstones, and I was advised by a Métis herbalist, Lori Snyder, about chickweed. It helped me so I didn't have to go for surgery, and my mind was blown. I started chasing Lori around Vancouver.

I started with the medicines reluctantly in the beginning. But when Maggie, my oldest daughter, was diagnosed with rheumatoid arthritis, I found a passion for it. It made me want to see, are there any plants and medicines that could help her, ease her pains, and maybe even cure her?

With Maggie, we were depending on Aleve a lot because it helped her pains, but we slowly got into devil's club and chaga tea. I'd get her up every day and make her drink a cup of tea. Then I discovered kids don't like taking medicine every day. She hated it with a passion.

So I started making it lighter, making a decoction so she'd only have to drink a little bit. She really pushed me in a direction of learning more, so I ended up training myself to make tinctures. I talked to Lori and another Indigenous herbalist, Cease Wyse, about the best ways to make it, what was best for her, what might work for her. Stinging nettle gave immediate pain relief, so I tried to get out and find it. I eventually brought it home to propagate, and now we have it out our front door.

Only this year did I realize that with this medicine journey, I'm actually being an Indigenous person. This is how we lived! This is how we did things! I'm learning in a circle with other women, other healers. Then I bring that home, and I am inadvertently teaching my kids. When we harvest, typically we all harvest together. They know about the drying, they've seen me doing the work, making the salves and the tinctures at home.

It's amazing, that realization: We have culture. This is tradition that we're living. Maggie is going to know this. I'm grooming her to be in charge of this knowledge, and when my time comes, it'll be passed down.

Dykstra: *I love that!*

Brown: I'm not so much a warrior, but I find that every barrier that comes up, I have to be really political about it. I'm the one who, when we go to a parks board meeting, says, "No, you have to do this; this is reconciliation. Rewilding is not just benefiting us for picking plants; it's benefiting children—children who don't even know what all kinds of flowers are. They go to the park, and it's just flat grass. How fun is that? Every kid loves to blow a dandelion. Where are they? Where can we find them?"

So I'm having an influence in different areas. I didn't realize that learning medicines would have an impact everywhere. Being called an influencer around land stewardship, I said, "What does that mean? Am I doing that? I don't think I'm doing that." But after I clearly understood what that meant, I realized I *am* doing that. And it's something to be proud of too, because it intertwines our culture of managing the lands and knowing what's best for what's around us.

Dykstra: *I know that the dominance of the Western medical system and the way that Indigenous families are subject to extra surveillance has impacted you supporting Maggie's health. Can you talk about that?*

Brown: I knew treating Maggie with our medicines was going to be a struggle for people at Children's Hospital. She's functioning well, but from day one, they've always pressured us: "We've gotta do *these* medicines, we can do them together if you want to, but she's gotta be on *these* medicines." We've negotiated through the whole process: "Give us time: she's doing teas, I've just started a tincture. We need to see if that works."

When she got on the tincture, everything seemed to be fine. Until this summer, she was taking her tinctures every day, and then she stopped and her pain started showing up again. She had two MRIs, and the second MRI showed a lot of inflammation.

And right away, they're coming at me: pressure, pressure, pressure. Trying to tell me we need to take their medicine because "this has become very serious." And I say, "But she's not taking her meds, so even if I wanted her to take your medicine, it's not gonna be any easier making her take it."

I want to focus on my medical plan of treatment in our cultural way. We still have a couple more steps to do and then see how it goes from there. And then the doctor said, "At some point I'm going to have to make a report to the ministry, because you're not taking our medicines. We think she's in serious pain and she needs interference."

It was a very tough day. I did a callout, a live feed, and connected to some supporters who had an employee with the Gitxsan family society up north call me. And it was very touching, because when she phoned, it turned out that she was my cousin. She's older than me, and we call her "Auntie." And she asked, "What is going on? What's happening?"

And I told her what they said to me. She advised me that we have every right to treat Maggie with our cultural medicines and nobody can interfere with that—especially if we've proven that it works.

Nothing's going to work overnight. The doctors said themselves their medicines may not even work. They may take three to six months to start working on her, but they don't give us the time. It's only been a year under diagnosis. It's all still new, and they're trying to fast-track us into something we don't want to do.

We don't heavily rely on what I call "colonized medicines." Very rarely would we take medicines for a headache. My kids don't take medicine, cough syrup, when they're sick; we have medicinal plants now that help with that. We have teas that we drink when we're feeling sick.

Being pressured is so traumatizing. But by the end of the day, I felt awesome having the confidence of my community behind me. I just had to put out one call, talk to one person. It spread out; everybody's concerned, and by the end of the day I got the support that I needed. So that was the most recent involvement with colonized society and that pressure. When things come up, I think about myself: "I can't believe you're doing this, but at the same time, I knew you would do it."

Dykstra: *How do you collect medicine living in the city, without a car, about a thousand miles from your traditional territory?*

Brown: With a group called the Resurfacing History project, we met with the Musqueam First Nation. Cease Wyse is part of the Squamish Nation, and she mentors us through all of this. We met one person from Tsleil-Waututh, and we got verbal permission to work and gather on these lands.

Because I don't have a car, I harvest totally by transit. I'm limited to access within the city. It's getting more and more difficult with the traffic and having to be aware of the exhaust around the plants, so we have to harvest strategically.

Going into medicines, I thought it was just going to be about my teas and tinctures. I didn't know until recently how big an impact it has on our entire environment. This revolves around my children and making sure they will continue to have access to these medicines. I feel a responsibility to encourage a garden format in schools, so I started talking with the school board. But in doing that and trying to manage that garden, I found barrier after barrier.

We have to get permission from the school board. We have to get permission from the city to move a water-access into the garden. We have to talk to the parks board, which usually comes on the school grounds and mows over everything at the time when we want to harvest. Red clover was one big thing that grew in abundance in the garden there, and it always seems when I want to come and harvest, here comes the mower. So it became very frustrating. I could go in there and throw a bunch of seeds around, but there's no communication between the organizations.

Now I'm going on this journey of influencing not only land management but Indigenous people and families and giving them knowledge. This is another important path. In the beginning I was reluctant to do it; I didn't want to share anything that I knew. But the teaching I've received from mentors is that we have to connect these bridges. In order for us to succeed, we need help from other people—to break down these barriers and make medicines more accessible to us.

And then it even goes into climate change discussions. This is important work that we're doing: not only that we're learning for our families but these are important cultural traditions that we're sharing and handing down to our kids. It's been amazing to see how far just picking plants can go.

And in picking plants, I need access. A lot of the places might be around train tracks or backyards. There are a few little gardens that are in open spaces that I can harvest from. But I can only go where transit can take me, so usually when I harvest, it takes an entire day.

Today I'm doing the Simon Fraser University project. They're going to train us to do photography so we can map everywhere we go out to harvest. I talk publicly about the spaces we get our foods from and our medicines. And about supporting each other and building community and connections, to make sure that these spaces are always available. Through this medicine, I'm making that change happen.

Dykstra: *Part of the reason for residential schools and of the reserve system was to move Indigenous people off their lands, which are the source of all kinds of connection, including wealth and resources. Can you talk about how that kind of economic displacement impacted your family?*

Brown: I think they've nearly succeeded in their assimilation. If the Truth and Reconciliation Commission hadn't happened, a lot of us would still be poor and stuck. Now we realize that they're doing this to have control over the lands and extract resources. Oppression is their main tool. They just want to keep us poor. There's huge racism against us for being Indigenous—this lie that we get money, we live tax-free, we get education free, we get all kinds of stuff free.

We want to live and trade with generosity and move away from money and this racist system that we live in now. It's going to take some time and be a difficult process because you need to have a job to pay the rent and you need to have a job to keep your kids in childcare. Otherwise, you're homeless.

Some elders refer to our reserve lands as concentration camps because you're forced to live just in this area. You can't go outside it. You can't build a house anywhere you want to. You live here and you can't do anything. I'm trying to encourage people to break down those barriers a little. Yes, you're stuck on the land, but you can still use your backyard. You can still grow some medicines, and you can still grow your own food. We're actually rich. We're a very wealthy society. We're just not wealthy in the sense of a hundred-dollar bill.

And we're talking about survival. If something seriously happened with the planet and we had an earthquake, or zombie apocalypse, we would be able to go climb in the mountains and go inland. We could live in the natural world that we were intended to live in. I can hunt. I can fish. I could teach my kids that. If we're sick, I now know the medicines that we need. We know how to grow food if we have to.

We know how to capture water if we need to. The system that we live in is so oppressive. Who goes out and buys bottled water? Almost everybody—when if you wanted to, you could just capture it. I'm just pretty confident that if anything goes down, we would be able to live.

Dykstra: *Maggie showed me some very cute photos of group costumes, and I know you do a lot of activities together as a family. Why is that so important to you?*

Brown: Again, it goes back to residential school and my mom not having that ability. At times, she attempted to have happiness during holidays, but she wasn't very successful. But I know when I do it, it's a family fun thing. It brings us closer together. Everybody has input.

Halloween is one of the things that we all decide together. I ask my children, "What do you guys want to be for Halloween? And do we have to buy costumes, or can we make them?" It's important to have that conversation. It helps them to deal with group conversations and having their own voice out in the world. It gives them confidence. It supports their imagination, and it bonds us together.

As soon as we're done, Halloween ideas start flying for the next year. And I thrive on that, because I can see how happy they are. And it makes me so happy in my heart, because these are cycles that I'm breaking. They're going to be healthier when they grow up and have their own children.

Dykstra: *We've talked about Maggie and Jack. Can you talk about how Jessica is in your family?*

Brown: Jessica is my older brother Chris's daughter. Chris and I never had a very close relationship because he was deep in his alcoholism. Jessica knows. That's one of the parenting things that I do with my kids: I don't lie to them. I tell them the truth about everything. In a way that says, "I don't want you holding this; this is not your responsibility to try to solve or try to make better. I'm just telling you because you need to be prepared." So Jessica knows I'm not her natural mom, and we've tried to work out a relationship with her real mom.

Her dad passed away a month after she was born as a result of alcoholism. Jessica was put in foster care for about six months. I had this other brother who really wanted to take her. I was kind of reluctant about being committed to looking after a child. But when he was denied by the ministry, I thought, "They're going to keep her in foster care. I don't want to lose her."

I put in my application to take her, but it was on a temporary basis. She spent some time with her mother, back with me, and with her aunt and her uncle before I got custody again. She saw a lot of violence and drug use during those years. And then coming home, she had no boundaries. She had no rules, being the only child in that adult world. She was hard to settle into the routine that we're used to.

So she knows where she comes from. I have her parents' pictures up on the wall. And I've always told her, and I told her mom, "Any time you want to come and see her, you're totally welcome. I only request that you're not under the influence. And you'll have to show the work in order to take her away for a day. It's going to be gradual. It has to be based on trust."

Jessica's mom went through residential school. She was actually in one of the last residential schools in British Columbia.

Dykstra: *And people say that residential schools are ancient history and survivors and their children should get over it.*

Brown: She has tons of trauma from that, which encourages her drug addiction. My brother passing away—that's more trauma. Her sister that she fully relied on died. Six months after that, Jessica's oldest brother, who was about twenty-four, passed away of a drug overdose. And her mom has dementia.

So in that short period, not only did Jessica go through a lot; her mom went through a lot. We see her on a downtown street corner every once in a while, and Jessica misses her sometimes. And I tell her, "We just gotta try to pray."

So last year, again with our medicines, we made traditional prayer ties with some cedar, a bit of devil's club, and some sage. We made about sixty of them and handed them out downtown. Our intention was on Christmas Day to go and see if Jessica's mom was down there, let her have that healing. Jessica wrote her mom a card and put her school picture in it, and we went to look for her, but she wasn't there.

But while we were down there, we handed out prayer ties to a lot of people. I haven't been down there in years, and it made me step back. All I could see was pain, depression, trauma, and hurt people. You know spirits are broken.

I was nervous to walk through that area with the kids, but I told them, "I'm gonna go wherever you want to go. I'll hand the prayer ties to whoever you think should take them." So they would pick, and we'd hand out a teaching as well: "Here's a prayer tie. When we gift it to you, it's from left hand to left hand. Left hand to left hand means it's from our heart to your heart and we're giving this in love."

A lot of the people had their drugs in their left hands, and they would hide them and be respectful to the kids, not letting them see that. A lot of them said that in that moment of the day, they really needed to hear our words and receive our gift. They really cherished that.

We walked around and ended up in Crab Park with a handful of our prayer ties. I guess a guy had stolen money from this woman, and she was there trying to get it back. He was going back in his tent, and she had a wood two-by-four. She was going beat him with it. And the kids were saying, "We should go give her one."

And I said, "Are you sure? Because she looks like she wants to fight somebody."

They said, "Yeah."

"Okay, if she gets aggressive to us, you guys need to step back behind me just in case. But we won't go there approaching her scared or anything."

So I approached her, saying, "Excuse me, I'm sorry to bother you, I don't want to interfere."

She saw the kids and immediately said, "I'm sorry. I'm so sorry."

I said, "It's okay. We're handing out prayer ties, and we have these last few left, and we want to gift you one."

She had the two-by-four in her hand. She dropped it and put her hands on Jackson's face and said, "I'm so sorry. You shouldn't see that." Jackson handed her the prayer tie, and she just started crying.

So when we handed out our last prayer tie, we talked about it. "What do you think about these people that are down here?" And Jackson and Jessica said, "They seem really sad."

I said, "They are. They're all lost in their own way, and they feel nobody loves them, I think. That's why they're here and in this state. So I think what we did was good. Do you think it was good?" They agreed. When we got home, we prayed for the people that we touched. And we decided that we're gonna talk about it every year, and if they feel up to it, we're going to go do it again. It's so simple. Just prayer ties.

Dykstra: *You're amazing.*

Brown: It felt amazing. I felt nervous being down there. I never went down there by myself because I was afraid. But the kids weren't. I just followed them, and they guided me.

In this little thing that we did, we viewed these people differently. They're not drug addicts. They're not what people call "crackheads." They're human beings that are hurt. They're sad. They need to be loved, and this was the way that we could give love to them in a respectful way.

And that's where the medicine has brought me: all over the place, involving everything we do.

Reflection Questions

1 How are medicine and health care part of my family's story?

2 What traditional ways in my own ancestral traditions would be helpful to revive for the sake of my children?

3 How am I working to heal my own trauma so as not to pass it down generationally?

15

Confessions of a Bad Movement Parent

Raising Children for Autonomy

Laurel Dykstra

Laurel Dykstra is an Anglican priest and author
who has been active in Christian movements for
social and ecological justice for more than thirty
years. With partner Julie and coparent Bruce,
Laurel is parent to twin seventeen-year-olds in
an urban core housing cooperative on Coast
Salish territory (Vancouver, British Columbia).
Author of *Set Them Free: The Other Side of
Exodus* (Wipf & Stock, 2012) and *Uncle Aiden*
(Babybloc, 2005) and the editor of *Bury the
Dead: Stories of Death and Dying, Resistance
and Discipleship* (Cascade, 2013) and *Liberating
Biblical Study* (Wipf & Stock, 2011), Laurel is
currently working on a book on spirituality and
interspecies loneliness in the Anthropocene era.

---

*Navigating Queer identities, disabilities, bodily autonomy, family, and
community, this chapter asks questions about sharing values between
generations. What do our parents intentionally and unintentionally give
us? How can we offer our children what we value and at the same time
support them to discover and choose their own deep integrity?*

Lost in Translation

Writing for a parenting anthology seems to imply that I have some insight to share—that I have done something right, whether accidentally or on purpose. Most of the time, I don't think this is true. Don't get me wrong: I think my children are amazing people. I genuinely like my kids—twins who just graduated from high school—and people I like, whose opinions I respect, like them too. Most days, I would say that parenting is something I have done pretty well, but I don't think that I am a good "movement" parent. I know parents—some of them contributors to this anthology—who seem to have conveyed a lot more of the movement life to their kids. Some are families whose lives have been steeped in the movement for generations.

I came to a network of faith-rooted social change movements as an adult because I went looking for a place where faith was lived large, where people were brave, where the consequences of what they believed made a difference in the world around them. I wanted to be around people who were tangibly giving their lives to the divine. The L'Arche, Catholic Worker, Pacific antiwar/antinuclear, and antiglobalization movements are the communities in which I began my family, the settings in which my kids were immersed for their first years.

I was arrested in a protest on Mother's Day while hugely pregnant. When they were small, my kids sported political patches on their onesies; were featured in rad parenting zines; lived in Catholic Worker hospitality houses; attended Earth First! Round River Rendezvous; napped in convergence spaces; went to rallies, actions, and political drag shows; and hoisted indecipherable poster-painted cardboard protest signs. But as near-adults, neither identifies with any of the political or spiritual movements that have nurtured and raised them.

When I think about my childhood and imagine what my parents tried to pass on—oblivious to my struggles, nightmares, and hopes—I guess the disconnect is not too surprising. That yawning, horrible gap between the world as adults imagine it and the contested spaces where children live separates every generation. The messages of my own brokenness and the desperate greed of the surrounding culture have influenced my children at least as much as the movement values I intended to impart.

And I wonder what and how much I missed and misconstrued in their lives. Parenting is the relationship in my life that I most strongly pursued and deliberately set out to achieve. It is the relationship that I have been most present to and have made my priority. It is sobering to think that what I have done best, most, and most intentionally landed so far from my goals.

If we weren't related, my dad would be the exact person I'd want on my apocalypse team or collective farm. Build a house, dig a well, plant a garden, midwife a goat, milk a cow, put up a fence, put down a dog, fix a broken appliance with only a few pieces left over—he was your guy. My father did a remarkable thing, deciding not to beat his kids the way he was beaten. But there was controlled hitting and always the threat of violence: "Don't cry or I'll give you something to cry about." And I've definitely liked much worse people better. But his combination of undiagnosed atypical neurological hardwiring, childhood trauma, alcoholism, and later-life head injuries made him a hard person for me to be around.

Yet I carry much of what I learned from him. Dirt smells really good. Pay attention, figure things out by observation, because you will be expected to competently do things that cannot be articulated: tie your shoes, find your way to the corner store, navigate schoolyard social hierarchy. Work hard and don't complain (much). Feelings don't change anything—however heartbroken or outraged you are. Any accomplishment by a daughter can be eclipsed by that of a son. I learned that if the first two or three steps of any task were clear (usually drawn on the inside of a cigarette package), you could act like it made sense and figure out the rest for yourself. I learned to appreciate a good meal.

From my mother, who I think was an extremely good parent, I learned to decline offers of generosity that could not be repaid: a car ride in the pouring rain, a dollar for washing a neighbor's windows. I learned to find sanctuary in the church and believe that I had a place in it. I learned to read books aloud to children. I learned that "being good" (whatever that meant) was extremely important. That disguising your skills and abilities was a form of good manners. And that there were questions you shouldn't ask.

If my parents had sat down before we were born to list the values they each hoped to pass on to my brother and me, there wouldn't have been a lot of overlap. Maybe work hard, share labor and produce with your neighbors, be frugal, persevere. Avoid the attention of people in authority. Quietly cover up the bad behavior of men with higher status. Be cheap. Smart matters. There are places and spaces where people like us don't belong.

As I live into the last half of my life (if my grandmother's life is the measure), or the last third (if we go by my parents' life span), some of these lessons are ingrained, some I openly flaunt, and others I am working to unlearn. Maybe it is not so surprising that what I hoped to give to my children got lost in translation. Maybe we are always communicating our experiences instead of our intentions.

Aims and Means

Looking back to my early years of parenting, it is hard to remember what I thought, wanted, or hoped for. My best guess is that I would have articulated my aims and means to my children like this:

Small humans, flannel-wrapped bundle of big eyes, slime, and razor fingernails. This little body is all yours. That means what goes on it, including those hideous, once-purple-quickly-gray, stained, polyester, flare-legged pants and that blue cable-knit sweater; felt-marker body art; the short dress that makes your grandmother frown; and that new, teeny-tiny rocket ship tattoo. Also what goes in it: tofu dogs, fluorescent-orange sweet-and-sour pork, sheets of roasted seaweed. Who touches it and how. Whether you know yourself to be boy, girl, or something else. All that is all up to you. Your choice. And how you let the rest of us know about those choices is up to you too.

Smash capitalism, babies. Make and share things. Resist materialism. Solve problems without violence. Ask a lot of questions and don't let anyone be the boss of you— not friends, not family, not popular culture. Threaded all through this manifesto and undergirding the community that holds you are stories and rituals, observances and relationships rooted in the Christian tradition that will be the warp and weft of the fabric of your lives.

If someday you see them on TV or read about them in books, know that those one-mum, one-dad, one-house families are not the only way to live. They're not even the way most people live. Community and how you make it matter.

There are things that I hope I have showed my children more than told them, but which of these are values of the movement or the things that I set out to impart? I am not sure. Nevertheless, I think our idiosyncratic takes on family, community, gender, disability, and school are things our haphazard parenting team and makeshift village have done well. Most of them have to do with autonomy and collectivity.

There is, in the ordination service in my church, a line that ordinands often resent or make fun of: "Will you do your best to pattern your life and that of your family in accordance with the teachings of Christ so that you may be a wholesome and holy example to your people?" There is a sense in which this is profoundly true of our family. This queer, gendery, three-parent, unschooling, co-op-living, Mad Pride crew is wholesome as shit.

Family Motto

When the girls were maybe four or five, their dad (my sperm donor), Bruce, read some parenting advice that said having a family motto is a good thing. So he brought the idea to the dinner table and we swiftly hit upon "I love you. You're weird. We like books." We still recite this motto from time to time, and it covers a lot.

I love you. We stand by one another, do things for one another. Each of us is secure in the bedrock of family solidarity, where we are fundamentally *for* one another. We see and recognize the fundamental goodness in one another. And that love is a basis for wonder at the world around us.

Love, love, love for the cat who came to us a bag of bones in a cardboard box needing syringe feeding every six hours—who expanded into twenty pounds of asthmatic sass in a pink harness and is now a cranky old man in fur pants. We love friends, cousins, the one-legged crow in the courtyard, tiny bioluminescent organisms at Mermaid Cove, and the steamed-bun store.

We live under social systems that reward conformity and compliance. I come from a family that emphasized hard work, accomplishment, and being good, and my own hardwiring tends toward binaries like good and bad, right and wrong. Against that backdrop, cultivating a family culture of recognizing joy, of unabashedly loving what you love, is no small thing.

You're weird acknowledges a host of differences in neurological wiring/processing, ability and disability, and lack of social graces. It also gives space and allows for gentle teasing of each family member's enthusiasms and nerd-doms: feeding spaghetti to tide pool crabs, obsessing over pencil-and-paper games, singing tuneless renditions of '80s pop hits, and delighting in shipwreck lore, musical theater, arcane knowledge of shark species, the history of the accordion, or biblical references to the cedar tree. All of which slides right into . . .

We like books. We are a collection of mostly introverts who engage with the world primarily through narrative. My mother collected illustrated children's books, and my partner still does. At a conservative estimate, the children heard well over a thousand hours of bedtime stories. Bruce regularly maxed out all our library card borrowing limits and interlibrary loan privileges.

Family holidays involve strategically packing of books that will please multiple readers, fiercely negotiating reading order, and making midweek outings to secondhand bookstores for reinforcements. Two of us are published authors. Bruce carries on a fine Christmas tradition (perhaps borrowed from a L'Arche assistant) of choosing and wrapping library books for family members. It shows you thought about them, you know what they might like, you trust them, and you value them over consumption.

Community

It has been important to me, who started out as a single (or at least strong majority) parent to have other competent adults around who can support my kids, fill in blanks, see in my blind spots, and be there for them in different ways. 'Cause I don't know anything about makeup, dance, music theater, spreadsheets, fashion, or sewing. But also because when you're parenting twins, you are always outnumbered. We've been able to give our kids an expanded and intentional family and, beyond that, a community.

My kids lived first in a Catholic Worker hospitality house with adults transitioning from the streets to more stable housing. Their fourth year was in a shared house with another family, and the following thirteen years in an urban core housing co-op in a rapidly gentrifying neighborhood. The first time I let them play in the courtyard unsupervised, they came in to tell me they met a girl and made a friend. Turns out she was a twenty-year-old shooting heroin in the alley next to the playground.

They have shared living space with me, their father, and my partner; had extended stays by godmother and grandmother; and had visits from traveling activists, guerilla plumbers, needle-exchange practitioners, and Indigenous land defenders. Upstairs is the tenants' rights organizer, across the courtyard live harm-reduction pioneers, and on the other side of the alley is an anticolonial migrant justice worker. The families adjacent to ours are deliberate and skilled in their practice of mentoring young people.

Much of what I think of as radical or countercultural was ambient or invisible to my kids growing up. When you're five, you don't notice or care that a flurry of phone calls and visitors with envelopes is actually a group of neighbors pulling together "the people's subsidy" so that a mum with kids can pay her housing charge. Neighbors knocking on the door to supply a meal, take an extra kid, borrow an ostrich egg, or an onion, or a bag of corduroy beards is just business as usual. Of course you can borrow the van to carry a totem pole, a coffin, a kayak, an electoral reform demonstration, the cast of a music theater production, folding chairs for the Black history presentation, cases of food to the Indigenous resistance camp.

Our kids know that family can look a lot of different ways. I remember at a birthday party a decade ago realizing there was not one child present from a stereotypical nuclear family. Our teeny guests lived with siblings, mothers, sperm donors, grandparents, godparents, aunts, stepparents. The only kid with one mum and one dad and siblings from a single marriage lived in a community house with two other families. Our social circle includes queer families, genderqueer families, multiracial families, families grown by adoption and fostering, long-term collective houses, and more recently, polyamorous families. I hope that we have shown our kids by who we are, who we love, and how we live that families are porous places, where you can both set limits and invite others in.

Gender

Over nearly two decades, during which much has changed in the gender awareness of our family and more broadly in the culture, it is instructive to think back about how we parented around gender and what we might have done differently. We used she/her/hers pronouns and also repeated the idea that "usually" girls had these anatomic features and boys these—but that you can't tell by looking and only *you* really know.

When they were small, the twins had clothes—onesies, dresses, pants, shirts—in all kinds of colors, with images ranging from flowers to dinosaurs and hand tools, made from flannel and fleece, denim and knits, some in satin with ribbons. As soon as they were able to indicate a preference, they were offered choices about what to wear, and by age three, they were choosing their own clothes even as they needed assistance getting them on. Early and adamantly, these choices tended toward pink and purple, horizontal stripes and animal prints—mostly girly, with a side of the hilarious, idiosyncratic, and practical: cowboy boots and rubber boots, capes, tutus, and hats with ears. Shorts and a tank top over leggings and long sleeves topped with a cardigan was the uniform for about a year.

Nobody in our family loves crowds, but we were regular participants in Pride events. An early photo shows both twins gazing up, way up, in wonder at Glamazon, a statuesque Seattle drag performer. Our circles included women farmers, doctors, blacksmiths, engineers, stay-at-home dads, and honorary guncles indulging delight in pretty dolls and party dresses. But our kids also saw a lot of assigned or assumed female people taking primary responsibility for care work and reproductive labor.

All my children's lives, out trans people with binary male or female identities have been part of our social world. But for the most part, because most of our real lives aren't made up of discussion of people's genitals—and because having a six-year-old loudly inquire, "Was this from when you were a *girl*?" isn't always safe or comfortable—we did not discuss our friends' gender identities with the children. Stigma is complicated, and our family has certainly participated in it. I think not wanting to use our friends as object lessons meant that we were quieter about gender diversity than we might have been when the twins were very young.

When a close family friend and age-peer of theirs came out as trans in junior high and a father in our church circles came out as a woman, I began a modest campaign of (consensually) outing other trans friends and acquaintances to our kids. The democratic alternative school that Harriet has just graduated from had been a low-key queer-positive space for years. But about five years ago, after two young teens transitioned to names, pronouns, and wardrobes that matched their gender identities, the school experienced a culture and demographic shift as other families came looking for a safer space for their kids. Kids promoted their school at trans community groups. Cis-identified students recognized aspects of their identity by seeing different expressions all around them. Of the most recent crop of high schoolers, easily 20 percent are trans, nonbinary, or gender nonconforming, and a number of parents have followed parallel trajectories.

Bodies and Brains

A godmother with multiple sclerosis, a father with bipolar disorder, grandparents living and dying with various cancers, depression, anxiety, diabetes—these are the official diagnoses of our extended household. We are pretty conversant with Mad Pride and Crip Liberation. But even though our co-op has ramps and elevators, our apartment has steps. Our family and neighborhood include people with all kinds of disabilities, diverse neurology, chronic health issues, and I hope by the ordinary business of going about our lives, we and our friends and neighbors have demonstrated the full inclusion, the awesome, resilient, inventive, badass, mundane, and ordinary facets of all kinds of bodies and brains. In our paid work, unemployment, unpaid work, and labors of love, I hope our family has shown its younger members that your job does not define you or give you value. But by keeping some of these things private, being more willing to talk about physical than mental health, failing to ask for help when we needed it, and putting emphasis on competence and self-sufficiency, we have also contributed to stigma and shame.

Lasting Values and Fears

Something our family has done well, if idiosyncratically, is to share our love of learning: our wild enthusiasm for thoughts, ideas, projects, and books. Before the twins were school-age, I lived in community or subsidized housing or did tag-team parenting and work that allowed our family to avoid both the expenses and challenges of childcare outside the home. Our days included plenty of art supplies and lots of exploring the small-scale world of wonder around them: beach, creek, garden, bones, leaves. In high school, Myriam was shocked to learn that her peers weren't raised on nature videos and that none of them could name more than five shark species. We read voraciously, collectively, and widely, entering deeply into book worlds—real, historical, and imaginary.

Both kids were deeply opposed to ideas that weren't their own and resisted formal learning from adults outside our broadly defined family. They were selectively mute, rarely speaking to adults outside the family before age seven. All of this made school quite challenging. So formal education in our family has included full French-language immersion, homeschooling, unschooling, a somewhat chaotic democratic alternative school where kids initiate classes, an urban core high school, musical theater, and an International Baccalaureate program.

As they leave high school, I wonder what of lasting value my kids have learned. They know the names of the Indigenous nations whose traditional territory we live on as settlers. I think they have been encouraged to love what they love. I believe we have demonstrated that learning and study, enthusiasm and curiosity are not just for school or for children and that it is a good thing to give time freely to what we value. But I fear that perfectionism and comparison to others have sometimes prevailed.

With our family, neighborhood, community, and school, I hope we have shown that adults make mistakes—and apologize and try again. And that we will support them and their decisions and choices. But I am afraid of so much. That we had too many juice boxes and car rides (things that I tend to think about as adaptations for accessibility). Faced with global climate crisis, I am afraid I have prepared them inadequately, for a world that doesn't exist anymore, and that my only insurance policy is relying on their, and my, place in the systems of inequity I say I oppose. (Probably should have read them more dystopian fiction and fewer of the Flower Fairies and ABC Mysteries books.) And that maybe, probably, I haven't made them tough enough. Adaptable enough. (And the joke's on me because, of course, I haven't *made* them at all.)

I am pretty sure I hovered too much, kept them too safe. Instead of expressing my deep love, my amazement that beings so wonderful and precious and capable could even exist, I may have communicated instead that they were fragile and incapable in a hostile world. I probably helped too much with schoolwork.

I fear the clash and harm that will come when they learn how far from universal the consent culture of their family and friends is. (I can't remember how old they were when I had to explain that it is not actually illegal for parents to post pictures of their kids on social media without permission.) I fear that in my own silence, reticence, privacy, I have failed to ignite in them a desire for a spiritual life. That it (everything) won't be enough.

Parenting Isn't Movement Building

A whole lot of my own identity and work is around the intersection of spirituality and politics, faith and justice, topics that hold little to no interest for my offspring. But I think—and in my best moments, I even believe—that good parenting is not about having children who are just like me. Parenting for autonomy means supporting children who are just like themselves.

While I wrote a first draft of this essay, Harriet didn't like the way a meeting at her school was going and stepped on stage to cochair with the chair of the school board and the district superintendent. She took over the mic to set some ground rules for respectful engagement and order of speakers. And she has some really incredible skills in directing and casting for theater that were painfully learned in negotiating issues of cultural appropriation, consent, and representation in terms of race, disability, and gender.

Myriam has the best work-life balance of anyone in the family. She attends to her schoolwork, but she makes relationships with her friends a priority. They balance friendship and romance, talk in pretty nuanced ways about issues of power, gender, race, and personality, and navigate stressful times together. I say she is not political, but her research topics and academic interests are all about justice issues: changing portraits of gay men in film, the Indigenous movement Idle No More, gentrification and displacement, the ban on gay blood donation, and queer characters in young adult lit.

I have had to learn that parenting isn't movement building. While I mentor youth and young adults in organizing and activism, social change work is not a family business that I have raised my children to take over. And for other parents coming up, my message is perhaps equal parts discouragement and encouragement: your values, what you do, what you believe in, what you struggle over in terms of parenting matters—but probably not as much or in the ways that you think.

We Turned Out Human

Laurel Dykstra's Daughter Myriam Responds

I just started university, and the thing I am learning about in all my classes is enculturation: the way in which we, as humans, are shaped wholly by culture, no matter where we are from. No child is born with a set of understandings of how to be or think. How a child is treated and who/what they are surrounded by as they develop are essential in a child's growth.

When I was learning how to walk and talk and interact with the world around me, I lived in a community-based environment where I learned how to trust and love and be. I grew up in an environment steeped in social justice and the knowledge that the way to change the world is to make your voice heard—be it through art or protests or politics.

After moving away, I went back to visit that house my sister and I lived in the first few years of our lives. I remember thinking that all the people living there were weird and wishing to go back home and see my "normal" friends who had homes and didn't go to protests wielding giant papier-mâché puppets. By leaving that environment and community at a very young age, I lost the sense of the values that were openly there and I became a different person as the cultural norms around me changed.

My mum is looking back now at how we were raised and wondering how she did—how all my parents did—and whether they could have done it all differently, to have my sister and me be more included in the movement. I don't believe that is a good way to measure parenting. Remember the good moments: protesting when we were babies and watching us take a bow at a sold-out show or moving into a university dorm. Those are the things we want you to think back on, not if you did it right and if your values were carried on through us.

I know where I came from and I know what is important to me. Whether or not I can clearly remember living in a community house in Tacoma, it is part of who I am. Our family is weird and wild and wonderful. Though they may not realize it, I do know what my parents have done for us. Instead of looking back on if you raised us right, look at the people we have become and are still becoming. You made me, and you made my sister, and look at what we are doing: living our lives, becoming more and more independent, taking the world by storm one way or another.

As I begin university, I am studying humanities, and in particular gender studies and social justice. I am not a religious person, and I doubt that I ever will be, but I strongly believe that I may rejoin some form of movement. So maybe my sister and I are not growing into the shell of past activists. Activism is changing. And we aren't going to grow up to become activists; we already are. We are not the people who are going to change the world when we grow up; we are the people who are changing the world right now.

We are the "military brats" of the social justice radical activist mom movement. We were radically parented to the best of your ability, and we turned out human.

Reflection Questions

1 How does parenting include both private, familial responsibilities and corporate, communal responsibilities?

2 How might I encourage cultures of "good enough" parenting or those that decrease parents' isolation and scrutiny and increase parents' sense of self and community care?

3 What are the values I most want to impart to young people? What do I love? How can we cultivate places where young people can deeply and unabashedly love what they love?

4 How can families and communities recognize and honor the parenting of nonbiological family members and nonparent contributors to children's lives?

5 How is what parents do influenced/impacted by a tendency to see children as products?

Conclusion

Blessings upon the Unraveling

Lydia Wylie-Kellermann

I come to the end of these pages with another ache in my depths. It is one of gratitude for all the stories, the struggles, the ideas, the permission to grieve, the acts of courage, and the lives that have loved.

Somehow each chapter has already seeped into my life. I find myself speaking phrases to my kids that are traced back to these pages. I find myself wanting to squander away time with my children. I want the men in my life to paint their toenails. I want to give library books as Christmas gifts. I want to talk about the end of capitalism over a game of Monopoly. I want to lay a picnic early in the spring with bread and cheese. I want to teach my kids to break rules such as "listen to your teacher." I want to spin webs of stories and listen to my kids' stories. I want to learn the medicinal herbs in my neighborhood. I want to record cassette tapes explaining to my toddler why I act for justice. I want to love the land where I stand. I want to expand the boundaries of family. I want to speak honestly with my partner when systems sneak into our marriage. I want to love my kids. I want my love to be big enough to scatter beauty and justice on all children, not just my own. I want a future for all of them, and their children's children, on this sweet Earth.

When my son Isaac stands under an umbrella of maple and oak trees, he moves with a quiet, deliberate slowness, keeping an eye out for movement or footprints laid upon the mud. In the spring, he takes off his shoes and wades into a foot of muck to convene with the bullfrogs. He knows creatures by name and sound and spirit. The times he spends among the trees are when his soul is most at ease. When I watch him watching a praying mantis, I think to myself, *This is who my child is meant to be.* His soul feels whole, his body grounded, and his heart alive.

This seven-year-old also has a clear and stubborn moral compass. He understands what comes out of the car mufflers and the factory stacks. Bottled water makes him angry. Driving a car makes him sad. Isaac and my partner, Erinn, bike to school (3.5 miles) almost every day. If I have to drive him in the car, his heart sinks at the thought of making pollution.

I thought about Isaac as I read Laurel Dykstra's chapter. I know they are right—parenting is not movement building. We do not raise kids to be just like us or hold the same political posture or to be numbers in a growing movement. Parenting is, however, loving fully the humans that stand before us and holding their hearts as we walk together into the unknown future.

Isaac is clear with us that he does not want us to drive any- where that we could get to by foot, bike, or public transportation. It is a rather novel suggestion when you live in the car capital of the world. It would not be easy, but the truth is that it would be possible.

The reality is, what he says is right. His instincts for caring for the earth regardless of convenience are good. Yet if I listen, if I really listen, and let him lead me, it will change the course of our lives. His many desires will force us to make hard choices and increase our daily work. But if we as a family do let his prodding heart change us, the empowerment he feels will give him courage and strength for the rest of his life. He will know that he, as a child, has power and that children are whole members of our community. And beyond that, as an adult when the myths are thrown in his face arguing that something is "too hard" or "impossible," he will forever know that it is possible to shift the patterns of life for the sake of justice. Perhaps the most powerful act of parenting I can do is to let him guide me.

We are living in a moment when so many of those normal patterns around us are shifting below our feet. I am finishing up editing this book two months into "shelter in place." The coronavirus has shaken us all. To the farthest corners of the earth, we are each holding tremendous grief and loss. The systems we thought were unbreakable are unraveling, and the injustice on which they were built is being exposed.

As I parent in this time, I realize how we are being confronted by so many of the elements addressed in these pages. So much is laid bare, from the deathly consequences from white supremacy to climate extraction to labor exploitation. People of color are disproportionately losing their lives in hospitals all around the country. Air pollution is a risk factor living in our lungs. For-profit health systems simply cannot save us. Grocery workers are dying of COVID-19 while making minimum wage, which cannot pay their rent. In my own city, thousands are living without running water when the only health advice is to "wash your hands."

But there is something else being exposed as well. We are seeing what is possible when we stop relying on capitalism and instead invest in our neighbors. There is a growing capacity of love, imagination, community, and blessed transformation. What a time to be alive. What a time for children to be listening and learning.

In my own neighborhood, we are gathering each day at five o'clock out in the street. Six feet away from one another, two dozen of us find a loving smile when we leave the kid chaos or silent loneliness of our homes. We distribute chalk to neighbors and make art. My four-year-old learned to ride a two-wheeler to the applause of the neighborhood. We drum. We sing. We ache. We despair. We laugh. I think this time with our neighbors is saving my kids.

We are also sitting down in our yards and letting our fingers entwine with the dandelions, comfrey, and violets. We bring these wild, edible plants to our pots and share recipes for immune boosting and respiratory medicines that we can share and store, trusting that we are one another's first line of support.

We are organizing ourselves for the long haul. Many of us have been rooting in this neighborhood for a long time. We've been getting to know our neighbors and earning one another's trust. In a way, it feels like we've been building community for so long in order to be ready for this very moment. We are checking in on elders. We are collecting and redistributing stimulus checks to those who were systemically denied theirs. We are planting gardens, canning jam, lending tools, parading on bicycles, and indeed, we are doing so much weeping.

Dear readers, through all this pain and uncertainty, each of us is holding these beloved children in our arms. How do we tend to their hearts? What are the stories and practices that will shape them? What can we teach them at home that they wouldn't learn in school? How do we share in the witness and experience of this unraveling time?

Let us embrace our children with everything we've got. Speak those family mottos. Cry. Scream. Learn how to care for ourselves and for strangers. Plant seeds. Love our elders. Name the truths. Dispose of systems of domination. Invest in community. Change course and live another way. Follow the lead of our wise children.

And so I leave you with this prayer, this hope, this longing as we each move forth into the ordinary and extraordinary moments of our lives.

May our children change us.
May we heed their cries and listen when their conscience
    speaks.
May we trust their hearts with the truth.
May we love them for the beings they are.
May our lives and words reject the addiction to systems of
    oppression.
May we put our bodies on the line, taking greater risks for
    justice.
May the work be done by hands that span the generations.
May the ancestors and rivers rise up to meet us.
May there be kindness and gentleness,

deep wailing and belly-aching laughter,
and always wonder and delight.
May we revel in our messy, beautiful humanness,
and may there be blessings upon our heads each time we go
    out the door.

Blessings on all the children and grandchildren whose lives summoned the words upon these pages.

Blessings on the children that you love. And on all those who will become part of the next chapters we all write together as we work to be the beloved community we are summoned to be.

Amen.

For Each Child That's Born

A Collective Poem

Collectively written by the contributors
September 8, 2019, Riverview, Michigan

For each child that's born,
Earth waits with her gift and wounds;
the creatures smile and weep;
the waters and winds rush and grow still.

A monarch unfolds its wings,
a beak breaks through its shell,
a tadpole finds legs,
and a million larvae take flight.

For each child that's born,
the Balance shifts to make room
and matter, time, and light bend around
the squalling cries.

For each child that's born,
an ancestor lives.
May this child ancestor be welcomed

as a previous, sacred being
by all of creation—
as a partner and friend.
May their landing be gentle
and our protection and love be fierce.

May this child be a joyful wake-up call to each of us
to live with gusto and stillness,
with righteous anger and creative action,
with tenderness and compassion.
May we say that your birth breathes life in each of us.

"Child, you walk on the precipice,
and teeter by the rush of the swollen river.

Listen.
Seek out understanding of others, of yourself,
of the divine universe.
Honor the Earth and wonder
at her magnificence.

You are a miracle!
A sacred promise.
love . . . and hope . . .
and holy imagination."

May each child find their place in a world of embrace,
stand by water and have the right stone
come into their palm—

smooth, flat, fitted to their dreams.
May they draw back their miraculous arms and lean forward,
unleashing what is theirs to give.
May that dream release and skip lightly
across the smooth surface that mirrors the sky in the earth,
and skip, and skip,
and may the sun catch the trees, the sky,
and the child,
and the entire earth clap their hands.

Guiding Values

In the midst of writing, most of the contributors gathered for a retreat in Michigan to share and reflect on one another's writings and to draft some shared commitments for this project. These are the commitments we named aloud and held as we wove this book together.

We all hold a commitment to the values of

- racial justice,

- climate justice,

- economic justice,

- disability justice,

- gender justice,

- sexuality justice,

- healing justice,

- land sovereignty/justice,

- nonviolence,

- beloved community,

- just plain love,

- intersection of identities/issues,

- value the freedom and integrity of children,

- healing wounds of our ancestors that we carry into our parenting,

- experimentation and creativity,

- vulnerability,

- resistance, and

- resilience.

We believe this book can

- hold the tension between interdependence and autonomy,

- hold the tension of what we stand for, what we want to create, and what we stand against, and

- be an experiment in dismantling white supremacy and patriarchy.

Acknowledgments

The only place to begin is with gratitude for the writers in this anthology. I love each of them. Some I have known since before I was born, some I've parented alongside, and others I've come to know through these pages. Within this circle are kindred spirits, visionary writers, and holy mentors. It is a gift to trust their hearts and imaginations.

Thanks to my kids, Isaac and Cedar, for your love, joy, and curiosity. You have made the questions in this book mean something to me. And there is never enough gratitude in the world for my partner, Erinn. Holding these questions together is a great joy in my life, and I trust that the answers we find could shift the course of our lives.

As I work on a book about parenting, I cannot help but bask in love for my own parents. My mom and dad told us the truth, lived a faith that embodied justice, and were committed to community in Detroit. I give thanks for my mom, who taught me through her dying about the sacredness of life and ingrained nonviolence in my bones. I give thanks for my dad as we continue to conspire together in everything from direct actions to book writing. And I give thanks for my sister, Lucy, who has been beside me through it all.

Acknowledgments

Thanks to Marcia Lee for bringing your wisdom, spirit, and ability to hold sacred space to the retreat for the contributors. Thank you to Joyce Hollyday for the brilliant support in editing and your constant love and support for my writing. Thank you, Kateri Boucher, for cooking food, reading, and helping me in the dark corners of editing. Thank you, Tommy Airey, for reading early drafts and for years of written conspiracies for community and justice.

Thank you to the Louisville Institute for giving us support to create this book in a way in which the process itself created community. Thank you to Broadleaf Books and Lisa Kloskin for hearing the need for such a book.

Gratitude for all the movements that are rising up from Detroit to wherever you are right now. For the resistance, the singing, the strategy, the stories, the power, the creation, and the community. For the elders and the ancestors. For the babies and children. And for those raising kids with lullabies of liberation.

For this land that holds our fragile, impermanent bodies; for the trees who give us breath; and for all the life with whom we share this time.

And for you, dear readers. You have been on my heart each day as this book took shape.

Notes

Introduction

xviii **grab hold of that arc:** "The arc of the moral universe is long, but it bends towards justice." Martin Luther King Jr., "Remaining Awake through a Great Revolution," speech, National Cathedral, Washington, DC, March 31, 1968.

A Note on Power, Process, and Accountability

xx **We wrote a list:** The list is found at the end of the book.

Chapter 2: Money

15 The quotes in this chapter are from personal interviews I conducted between July 23 and October 31, 2019.

Chapter 3: Education

33 Akilah S. Richards, *Fare of the Free Child*, podcast, https://www.raisingfreepeople.com/podcast/.

33 The quotes in this chapter are from personal interviews I conducted between May and July 2019.

35 **"You may be asking":** This text may be found in the "Schools That Work for Us" PDF available for download at "Schools That Work for Us," Hearing Youth Voices, accessed August 27, 2020, https://www.hearingyouthvoices.com.

39 **"the standardization covenant":** Todd Rose, *Dark Horse: Achieving Success through the Pursuit of Fulfillment* (New York: HarperOne, 2018).

41 **Some evidence even suggests:** Peter Gray, "How Early Academic Training Retards Intellectual Development," *Psychology Today*, June 3, 2015, https://www.psychologytoday.com/us/blog/freedom -learn/201506/how-early-academic-training-retards-intellectual -development.

45 **"It is not a coincidence":** "Schools That Work for Us."

Chapter 4: Where to Live

61 **"I was enclosed":** Thomas Merton, *The Seven Storey Mountain: An Autobiography of Faith* (New York: Harcourt, 1948), 372.

62 **We can tell:** Allegra di Bonaventura, *For Adam's Sake: A Family Saga in Colonial New England* (New York: Liveright, 2014).

Chapter 5: Spirituality

69 **"The master's tools":** Audre Lorde, "The Master's Tools Will Never Dismantle the Master's House," in *Sister Outsider: Essays and Speeches* (Berkeley, CA: Crossing Press, 2007), 110–14.

69 **"what love looks like":** Cornel West, "Cornel West: Justice Is What Love Looks Like in Public," YouTube, April 17, 2011, sermon, Howard University, Washington, DC, 2011, https://www.youtube .com/watch?v=nGqP7S_WO6o.

75 **I borrowed heavily:** Gertrud Mueller Nelson, *To Dance with God: Family Ritual and Community Celebration* (Mahwah, NJ: Paulist Press, 1986).

81 **We listened to chants:** In July 2014, Eric Garner was killed by police in New York. He screamed, "Stop, I can't breathe," while police officers held him in a chokehold until he died.

Chapter 6: Moving beyond Normativity

85 **la facultad:** Gloria Anzaldúa, *Borderlands / La Frontera: The New Mestiza* (San Francisco: Aunt Lute, 1987), 60.

Chapter 7: Raising Antiracist White Kids

104 **failing to give:** Beverly Daniel Tatum, *"Why Are All the Black Kids Sitting Together in the Cafeteria?": And Other Conversations about Race* (New York: Basic, 1997), 6.

107 **Oluo digs into:** Ijeoma Oluo, *So You Want to Talk about Race?* (New York: Seal Press, 2018).

Chapter 8: Resisting Patriarchy

119 **Like the author:** bell hooks, *Feminism Is for Everybody* (Cambridge, MA: South End, 2000), ix.

121 **Nathan read books:** Robin Wall Kimmerer, *Braiding Sweetgrass: Indigenous Wisdom, Scientific Knowledge* (Minneapolis: Milkweed Editions, 2013); and Alexis Pauline Gumbs, ed., *Revolutionary Mothering: Love on the Frontlines* (Oakland, CA: PM Press, 2016).

Chapter 9: Ableism

136 **She hesitated:** Janice Fialka, *What Matters: Reflections on Disability, Community and Love* (Toronto: Inclusion, 2016).

Chapter 11: The Power of Story

167 **The first book:** Randy Woodley, *The Harmony Tree: A Story of Healing and Community* (Victoria, British Columbia: Friesens, 2016).

Chapter 12: Building Community

188 **in Taiwan, the motherbaby:** *Motherbaby* is the idea that although the baby has come out of the womb, in the fourth trimester, the mother and baby are still spiritually/emotionally interconnected. For more, see Kimberly Ann Johnson, *The Fourth Trimester: A Postpartum Guide to Healing Your Body, Balancing Your Emotions, and Restoring Your Vitality* (Boulder, CO: Shambhala, 2019).

189 **As named by:** "What Is Healing Justice," Healing by Choice!, accessed November 25, 2019, https://www.healingbychoicedetroit .com/what-is-healing-justice.

Chapter 13: Risk and Resistance

198 **"I didn't want to":** Jeanie Wylie-Kellermann, "Within a Communion of Children," *On the Edge* 12, no. 1 (Winter 1987): 1.

200 **"Bill and I":** Wylie-Kellermann, 1.

201 **Witness for Peace:** See Ed Griffin Nolan, *Witness for Peace: A Story of Resistance* (Louisville, KY: Westminster / John Knox Press, 1991).

202 **One of our number:** "Charlie Liteky, 85, Dies; Returned Medal of Honor in Protest," *New York Times*, January 23, 2017.

203 **as if bad parenting:** Another account of this story may be found in Bill Wylie-Kellermann, *Dying Well: The Resurrected Life of Jeanie Wylie-Kellermann* (Detroit: Cass Community, 2018), 43–46.

205 **Jeanie had done something:** See Jeanie Wylie-Kellermann, "Anatomy of a Strike," *The Witness* 79, no. 9 (September 1996): 10–15; and Bill Wylie-Kellermann, "Readers before Profits: The Detroit Newspaper Strike," *Sojourners* (January/February 1996), https://sojo.net/magazine/january-february-1996/readers-profits.

209 **"woman clothed":** Rev 12:1 ESV.

209 **"I'm grateful for":** See Bill Wylie-Kellermann, "O Holy Nightmare," in *Seasons of Faith and Conscience: Explorations in Liturgical Direct Action* (Eugene, OR: Wipf & Stock, 2008), 140–48.

209 **Maybe it's not even:** Lydia Wylie-Kellermann, "Elders and Children Lay Their Hands upon Us Now," *Geez*, September 20, 2019.

For Each Child That's Born

255 We wrote this poem after singing Sweet Honey in the Rock's "For Each Child That's Born."

Further Resources

I f you are hungry to dive deeper into more stories and texts around these areas of justice and parenting, here are some recommendations offered by the contributors. (Plus I threw in some of their own books, because they are amazing.)

General Recommendations
for the Intersection of Parenting and Justice

Revolutionary Mothering: Love on the Front Lines
    Edited by Alexis Pauline Gumbs (PM Press, 2016)

We Live for the We: The Political Power of Black Motherhood
    By Dani McClain (Bold Type, 2019)

Parenting for Peace and Justice
    By James McGinnis and Kathleen McGinnis (Orbis, 1990)

Sustaining Spirit: Self-Care for Social Justice
    By Naomi Ortiz (Reclamation, 2018)

Parenting Forward: How to Raise Children with Justice, Mercy, and Kindness
    By Cindy Wing Brandt (Eerdmans, 2019)

What Makes a Family? Infertility, Masculinity, and the Fecundity of Grace, *by Nick Peterson*

On My Way Home: A Memoir of Kinship, Grace, and Hope
    By Sharon L. McDaniel (A Second Chance, 2017)

Chasing Kites: One Mother's Unexpected Journey through Infertility, Adoption, and Foster Care
    By Rachel McCracken (self-pub., Amazon, 2017)

Heavy: An American Memoir
    By Kiese Laymon (Scribner, 2019)

Listening to My Body
    By Gabi Garcia (Skinned Knee Publishing, 2017)

Money: Nurturing a Family Culture of Generosity and Justice, *by Susan Taylor*

The Biblical Vision of Sabbath Economics
    By Ched Myers (Tell the Word, 2002)

Sabbath Economics: Household Practices
    By Matthew Colwell (Tell the Word, 2007)

Education: Learning at the Speed of Trust, *by Kate Foran*

"A Thousand Rivers," "Occupy Your Brain," "On the Wildness of Children," "Children, Learning, and the 'Evaluative Gaze' of School"
    Essays by Carol Black
    http://carolblack.org

The Brave Learner: Finding Everyday Magic in Homeschool, Learning, and Life
By Julie Bogart (TarcherPerigee, 2019)

Pedagogy of the Oppressed, 30th anniversary edition
By Pablo Freire (Continuum, 2000)

Teaching to Transgress: Education as the Practice of Freedom
By bell hooks (Routledge, 1994)

We Want to Do More Than Survive: Abolitionist Teaching and the Pursuit of Educational Freedom
By Bettina Love (Beacon, 2019)

Project-Based Homeschooling: Mentoring Self-Directed Learners
By Lori McWilliam Pickert (self-pub., CreateSpace, 2012)

Fare of the Free Child (podcast)
By Akilah S. Richards
https://www.raisingfreepeople.com/podcast/

Where to Live: Putting Down Roots and Being Known, *by Frida Berrigan*

It Runs in the Family: On Being Raised by Radicals and Growing into Rebellious Motherhood
By Frida Berrigan (OR Books, 2015)

For Adam's Sake: A Family Saga in Colonial New England
By Allegra di Bonaventura (Liveright, 2013)

Radical Homemakers: Reclaiming Domesticity from a Consumer Culture
By Shannon Hayes (Left to Write, 2010)

Liturgy of the Ordinary: Sacred Practices in Everyday Life
By Tish Harrison Warren (IVP, 2016)

Geez magazine, contemplative cultural resistance
https://www.geezmagazine.org

"The Pequot Massacre," Zinn Education Project
https://www.zinnedproject.org/news/tdih/pequot-massacre/

Spirituality: Entrusting Our Children to the Path, *by Dee Dee Risher*

To Dance with God: Family Ritual and Community Celebration
By Gertrud Mueller Nelson (Paulist Press, 1986)

The Soulmaking Room
By Dee Dee Risher (Upper Room Books, 2016)

Moving beyond Normativity: Family as a Haven for Authenticity, Self-Expression, and Equity, *by Jennifer Castro*

Borderlands / La Frontera: The New Mestiza
By Gloria Anzaldúa (Aunt Lute, 2012)

The Enneagram Made Easy: Discover the 9 Types of People
By Renee Baron and Elizabeth Wagele (Harper, 1994)

Black Dove: Mamá, Mi'jo, and Me
By Ana Castillo (Feminist Press at CUNY, 2016)

Massacre of the Dreamers: Essays on Xicanisma
   By Ana Castillo (Plume, 1995)

A Thinking Woman's Guide to a Better Birth
   By Henci Goer (TarcherPerigee, 1999)

The Sacred Enneagram: Finding Your Unique Path to Spiritual Growth
   By Christopher L. Heuertz (Zondervan, 2017)

Further recommendations include anything by Brené Brown, memoirs from Mary Karr, poetry by Andrea Gibson, and the art of Frida Kahlo

Raising Antiracist White Kids: Some Rules Need to Be Broken, *by Jennifer Harvey*

Raising Antiracist Kids: An Age by Age Guide for Parents of White Children
   By Rebekah Gienapp (self-pub., 2019)

Raising White Kids: Bringing Up Children in a Racially Unjust America
   By Jen Harvey (Abington, 2018)

Resisting Patriarchy: Messy, Beautiful Interdependence, *by Sarah and Nathan Holst*

The Will to Change: Men, Masculinity, and Love
   By bell hooks (Washington Square, 2004)

Ableism: Opening Doors and Finding Transformation, *by Janice Fialka*

What Matters: Reflections on Disability, Community & Love
By Janice Fialka (Inclusion, 2016)

Toast
By Laurie Foos (GemmaMedia, 2018)

Intelligent Lives, documentary
Directed by Dan Habib (2019)

Being Realistic Isn't Realistic: Collected Essays on Disability, Identity, Inclusion and Innovation
By Emma Van der Klift and Norm Kunc (Tellwell Talent, 2019)

The Sibling SLAM Book: What It's Really like to Have a Brother or Sister with Special Needs
Edited by Don Meyer (Woodbine House, 2005)

Autism in the Family
By Robert Naseef (Brookes, 2015)

My Heart Can't Even Believe It: A Story of Science, Love and Down Syndrome
By Amy Silverman (Woodbine House, 2016)

Far from the Tree: Parents, Children, and the Search for Identity
By Andrew Solomon (Scribner, 2013).

Honoring Earth: Healing from the Carceral Mind and Climate Crisis with Joyful Interconnectedness, *by Michelle Martinez*

The Politics of Trauma: Somatics, Healing and Social Justice
By Staci K. Haines (North Atlantic, 2019)

The Power of Story: Subversive Lessons from Grandmother Oak, *by Randy Woodley*

The Harmony Tree: A Story of Healing and Community
By Randy Woodley (Friesens, 2016)

Shalom and the Community of Creation: An Indigenous Vision
By Randy Woodley (Eerdmans, 2012)

Building Community: Choosing Life in the Certainty of Death, *by Marcia Lee and en sawyer*

Standing by Words: Essays
By Wendell Berry (Counterpoint, 2011)

The Next Great American Revolution: Sustainable Activism for the Twenty-First Century
By Grace Lee Boggs (University of California Press, 2012)

Emergent Strategy: Shaping Change, Changing Worlds
By adrienne maree brown (AK Press, 2017)

American Revolutionary: The Evolution of Grace Lee Boggs
Documentary produced by Grace Lee (2014)

Let Your Life Speak: Listening for the Voice of Vocation
By Parker Palmer (Jossey-Bass, 1999)

The Unsettlers: In Search of the Good Life in Today's America
By Mark Sundeen (Riverhead, 2018)

Risk and Resistance: The Cost and Gifts to Our Children, *by Bill Wylie-Kellermann*

Bury the Dead: Essays on Death and Dying, Resistance and Discipleship
Edited by Laurel Dykstra (Wipf & Stock, 2013)

Dying Well: The Resurrected Life of Jeanie Wylie-Kellermann
By Bill Wylie-Kellermann (Detroit: Cass Community, 2018)

Seasons of Faith and Conscience: Explorations of Liturgical Action
By Bill Wylie-Kellermann (Wipf & Stock, 2008)

How Do I Heal the Future? Reclaiming Traditional Ways for the Sake of Our Children, *an Interview with Leona Brown by Laurel Dykstra*

Trudy's Rock Story
By Trudy Spiller (Medicine Wheel Education, 2017)

Gifts of the Land: Lílwat Botanical Resources
Lands and Resources Department (2017)

Confessions of a Bad Movement Parent: Raising Children for Autonomy, *by Laurel Dykstra*

Kids on Strike!
By Susan Campbell Bartoletti (HMH Books for Young Readers, 2003)

Stay Solid: A Radical Handbook for Youth
By Carla Bergman (AK Press, 2013)

Curious Kids Nature Guide: Explore the Amazing Outdoors of the Pacific Northwest
By Fiona Cohen (Little Bigfoot, 2016)

Uncle Aiden
By Laurel Dykstra (Babybloc, 2005)

Teenage Liberation Handbook: How to Quit School and Get a Life and Education
By Grace Llewellyn (Lowry House, 1998)

Bibliography

Anzaldúa, Gloria. *Borderlands / La Frontera: The New Mestiza*. San Francisco: Aunt Lute, 1987.

Boggs, Grace Lee. "Seeds of Change." PBS, August 31, 2007. http://www.pbs.org/moyers/journal/test_blogs/2007/08/seeds_of_change.html.

brown, adrienne maree. *Emergent Strategy: Shaping Change, Shaping Worlds*. Chico, CA: AK Press, 2017.

di Bonaventura, Allegra. *For Adam's Sake: A Family Saga in Colonial New England*. New York: Liveright, 2014.

Fialka, Janice. *What Matters: Reflections on Disability, Community and Love*. Toronto: Inclusion, 2016.

Gibran, Kahlil. *The Prophet*. New York: Alfred A. Knopf, 1923.

Gray, Peter. "How Early Academic Training Retards Intellectual Development." *Psychology Today*, June 3, 2015. https://www.psychologytoday.com/us/blog/freedom-learn/201506/how-early-academic-training-retards-intellectual-development.

Gumbs, Alexis Pauline, ed. *Revolutionary Mothering: Love on the Frontlines*. Oakland, CA: PM Press, 2016.

Habib, Dan, dir. *Intelligent Lives*. Documentary. New York: 2018.

Healing by Choice! "What Is Healing Justice." Accessed November 25, 2019. https://www.healingbychoicedetroit.com/what-is-healing-justice.

Hearing Youth Voices. "Schools That Work for Us." Accessed August 27, 2020. https://www.hearingyouthvoices.com.

hooks, bell. *Feminism Is for Everybody*. Cambridge, MA: South End, 2000.

Johnson, Kimberly Ann. *The Fourth Trimester: A Postpartum Guide to Healing Your Body, Balancing Your Emotions, and Restoring Your Vitality*. Boulder, CO: Shambhala, 2017.

Kimmerer, Robin Wall. *Braiding Sweetgrass: Indigenous Wisdom, Scientific Knowledge*. Minneapolis: Milkweed Editions, 2013.

King, Martin Luther, Jr. "Nonviolence: The Only Road to Freedom." Speech, May 4, 1966.

———. "Remaining Awake through a Great Revolution." Speech, National Cathedral, Washington, DC, March 31, 1968.

Lorde, Audre. "The Master's Tools Will Never Dismantle the Master's House." In *Sister Outsider: Essays and Speeches*, 110–113. Berkeley, CA: Crossing Press, 2007.

Merton, Thomas. *The Seven Storey Mountain: An Autobiography of Faith*. New York: Harcourt, 1948.

Nelson, Gertrud Mueller. *To Dance with God: Family Ritual and Community Celebration*. Mahwah, NJ: Paulist Press, 1986.

New York Times. "Charlie Liteky, 85, Dies; Returned Medal of Honor in Protest." January 23, 2017.

Nolan, Ed Griffin. *Witness for Peace: A Story of Resistance*. Louisville, KY: Westminster / John Knox, 1991.

Oluo, Ijeoma. *So You Want to Talk About Race?* New York: Seal Press, 2018.

Richards, Akilah S. *Fare of the Free Child*. Podcast. https://www.raisingfreepeople.com/podcast/.

Rose, Todd. *Dark Horse: Achieving Success through the Pursuit of Fulfillment*. New York: HarperOne, 2018.

Rossen, Paul, dir. *Through the Same Door: Inclusion Includes College*. 2006. DVD. http://www.throughthesamedoor.com/pages/buydvd.html.

Tatum, Beverly Daniel. *"Why Are All the Black Kids Sitting Together in the Cafeteria?": And Other Conversations about Race*. New York: Basic, 1997.

West, Cornel. "Cornel West: Justice Is What Love Looks Like in Public." YouTube, April 17, 2011. Sermon, Howard University, Washington, DC, 2011. https://www.youtube.com/watch?v=nGqP7S_WO6o.

Woodley, Randy. *The Harmony Tree: A Story of Healing and Community.* Victoria, British Columbia: Friesens, 2016.

Wylie-Kellermann, Bill. *Dying Well: The Resurrected Life of Jeanie Wylie-Kellermann.* Detroit: Cass Community, 2018.

———. "O Holy Nightmare." In *Seasons of Faith and Conscience: Explorations in Liturgical Direct Action*, 140–48. Eugene, OR: Wipf & Stock, 2008.

———. "Readers before Profits: The Detroit Newspaper Strike." *Sojourners* 25, no. 1 (January/February 1996). https://sojo.net/magazine/january-february-1996/readers-profits.

Wylie-Kellermann, Jeanie. "Anatomy of a Strike." *The Witness* 79, no. 9 (September 1996): 10–15.

———. "Within a Communion of Children." *On the Edge* 12, no. 1 (Winter 1987): 1.

Wylie-Kellermann, Lydia. "Elders and Children Lay Their Hands upon Us Now." *Geez*, September 20, 2019, 6.